Devil's Trap Podcast
presents
LORE AND MORE

Season 1

By Liz Waddell

For Diana, who has sat through each and every one of these stories, no matter how gross, scary, or bizarre.

Introduction

I am often asked where the idea for Devil's Trap Podcast came from. Honestly, some of it was a bit of the COVID pandemic insanity, but mostly it was because the long-running TV show Supernatural was ending after fifteen seasons, and I was feeling sad. I didn't want to let it go. I also really wanted to finally get my friend Diana to watch the show so we could talk about it. Then, when deciding on formats, including Lore made sense given my research background and my love for the occult and the high strange. A part of me knew that with so many episodes, some creativity would be called for, and that it would be a challenge to do a new topic every week, but I also knew a deep dive into a new topic every week works really well with my ADHD squirrel brain. I've enjoyed revisiting these topics and adapting them for the written page, and hope that you do too.

White Rock Lake

Season 1, Episode 1

Title: Pilot

Dropped: November 25, 2020

Oh, the first episode of Supernatural and Devil's Trap Podcast. So I chose the lore for this one because the monster of the week was a Lady in White. And also because White Rock Lake is near Diana, and she is super afraid of ghosts. That is what good friends do.

White Rock Lake is a man-made reservoir situated just northeast of downtown Dallas, Texas. Since its inception, it has been the backdrop for a haunting involving a mysterious woman. The first documented account emerged in 1943, when Anne Clark published "The Ghost of White Rock" in the Texas Folklore Society's publication, "Backwoods to Border."

The story follows the classic woman-in-white motif: a young couple parked by the lake when, as they switched on their headlights to leave, a young girl in white appeared before them. They listened to her recount a tragic tale about her boat capsizing and kindly offered her a ride home. Following the address she provided in Oak Cliff, they arrived only to find she had vanished. The only evidence of her presence was a damp rumble seat. When they knocked on the door of the house, a man answered and revealed that his daughter had drowned in White Rock Lake just weeks prior.

Frank X. Tolbert, in his book "Neiman-Marcus, Texas: The Story of the Proud Dallas Store," spins another variant from the perspective of the store directors of display, Mr. and Mrs. Maloy. The girl in this story is a beautiful blonde who again appeared in headlights, in a wet white dress. According to Tolbert, Mrs. Malloy said, "Stop, Guy. That girl seems to be in trouble. She must have fallen into the lake. Her dress is wet. Yet you can tell that it is a very fine dress. She certainly got it at the Store." Which does make you wonder if they would have stopped if her dress looked like it came from Sears. The couple lets the girl in her car, and she gives them an address in Lakewood. When the car starts, the girl vanishes, leaving behind a wet seat. What does this ghost have against people's upholstery? The couple drove to the address anyhow and were informed that the blonde daughter of the house, who of course, wore nothing but Neiman-Marcus clothes, had died when she fell off the pier at White Rock Lake. If this was a publicity stunt, it was a strange one.

If you look for facts, there were some cases of women drowning at White Rock Lake. The earliest was in 1927 when Hallie End Gaston drowned after her boat capsized. Another tragedy occurred in 1934 when a small plane crashed in the lake, leaving no survivors. There were at least two cases of suicide by drowning in 1935 and 1942. Could any of these be the ghosts who haunted the road to the lake for so long?

The hauntings became such a local legend that a well-known psychic from Dallas, Mary King, conducted a séance to put the spirits to rest. According to the YouTube channel

Savage Mister, the sightings stopped after this event.

Select Sources

Another possible White Rock Lake drowning - Lakewood/East Dallas https://lakewood.advocatemag.com/2014/05/21/another-possible-white-rock-lake-drowning/

Haunted Rooms https://www.hauntedrooms.com/texas/ghost-hunts/the-original-white-rock-lake-ghost-hunt-dallas

Lady of the Lake - For the Love of the Lake https://whiterocklake.org/white-rock-lake/lady-of-the-lake/

White Rock Lake | The Lady of the Lake | Ghost Texas (https://ghosttexas.com/white-rock-lake-the-lady-of-the-lake/

the-Woman-in-White-A-Legend https://exemplore.com/paranormal/The-Woman-in-White-A-Legend

Why are there so many ghost stories about a woman in white https://io9.gizmodo.com/why-are-there-so-many-ghost-stories-about-a-woman-in-w-5851037

Wendigo, Swift Runner, and Jack Fiddler

Season 1, Episode 2

Title: Wendigo

Dropped: December 3, 2020

Sam and Dean battled with a wendigo, so the choice for the lore was obvious. There's a clear difference between the traditional understanding of the wendigo and its portrayal in the episode, as well as in pop culture more broadly (e.g., the man with a deer-head image). While researching the wendigo, I read the stories of Swift Runner and the Fiddlers and felt the need to share.

Wendigo

There is documentation of the wendigo phenomenon dating back centuries. The first written occurrence was recorded in Jesuit letters in the 17th century, around the same time as the European Werewolf Trials[1], and

---

[1] DTP covers the Werewolf Trials in Season 2, Episode 5 "Heart".

these trials may have influenced some of the descriptors.

There are many variations of the name and its spelling; you will see "wendigo" or "windigo" most often. According to Monstrum.com, there are at least 37 ways to spell it. We will use *wendigo* for continuity's sake.

Within traditions of the Algonquian tribes native to the Great Lakes, eastern Canada, and the northern US, a wendigo is a cannibalistic monster that preys on the vulnerable, particularly those who are socially isolated. In some versions, it is a physical creature, but most often, it is a person possessed after being driven mad by cannibalism and loneliness. Candidates include individuals who suffer from loneliness, greed, or weakness. Or people who are attacked in their dreams by magical warfare or curses. Or people who eat other people.

Looks

Because of the many variations of the legend, there are no definitive descriptions of a wendigo. The most common traits are: gigantic in height (up to 15 feet tall), super thin, made of ice, matted hair, and decaying skin. In some versions, they eat off their own lips and other parts because they are so hungry.

Powers

Wendigos almost always have supernatural powers to help hunt victims - things like strength, powerful eyesight, a strong sense of smell, or the ability to navigate territory quickly, particularly snow and water.

How to kill

Wendigos can be killed by weapons, extracting the heart and burning it, or, in some legends, spiritual leaders can expel the spirit through rituals, sparing the possessed without killing them.

Swift Runner

In the 1800s, there lived a man named Ka-Ki-Si-Kutchin, more commonly known as Swift Runner, who was a Cree from what is now central Alberta. Although once thought of as an upstanding man, he was expelled from the community for causing trouble.

He took his family: wife, mother (or mother-in-law, depending on the version), brother, and six children out to a winter camp. After time passed, he made his way back to the community, but alone. His in-laws became suspicious and went to the local authorities, the Mounties, to seek help in determining what happened to their family. The Mounties could not find Swift Runner's camp.

Swift Runner turned himself into the Mounties in the spring and when questioned said, "My wife killed herself, and the kids all starved to death." The Mounties could see for themselves that Swift Runner himself didn't appear malnourished, so they asked to be taken to his camp to look around. At the camp, they discovered the family's remains.

Questioned again, Swift Runner said his dreams were haunted by a wendigo spirit who overpowered him and drove him to consume everything. Then Swift Runner confessed to a French missionary that he stabbed his ten-year-old child while the rest of the family was out foraging. When they returned, he told them the child had succumbed to starvation. As the winter and lack of food continued, the eldest son died from starvation. This additional grief caused the wendigo spirit to return to Swift Runner, and he murdered his wife and three girls. Swift Runner was left with just his youngest son, who survived with him until the Spring thaw, but not long after, the wendigo arose again within Swift Runner. During his confession, he did not say what happened to either his brother or mother.

Escorted to Fort Saskatchewan, Swift Runner's trial began on August 8, 1879. Among his jury were three "English-speaking Cree", four men who were "well up in the Cree language," and a Cree translator. They also brought in a Cree language expert to ensure Swift Runner understood what was said. At the trial's conclusion, he was convicted and sentenced to hang, becoming the first person executed in this territory. There was no infrastructure for executions, and gallows had to be constructed. There was also just general fuckery in how the hanging day, December 20, 1879, went. First, it was cold even for Canada (-40 degrees Fahrenheit), and the crowd who came to witness it were so freezing they took part of the gallows trap and burned it for warmth. So the gallows had to be rebuilt, causing delays to the execution. The "hangman" had never committed an execution before, so that also added to the time, but eventually he hanged Swift Runner. Swift Runner's last words were, "I'm no longer a man."

Jack Fiddler

The area's natural landscape cut off the Northwestern Ontario region's indigenous population from major trade routes until the Hudson Bay Company reopened the Trading Post at Island Lake in Northwestern Ontario in 1864. Initially, the Trading Post brought some much-needed financial life to the people of the region, but then decades of resource depletion and famine followed.

Five clans inhabited the area: the Sucker, Pelican, Crane, Sturgeon, and Caribou. The Sucker Clan was led by Peemeecheekag, also known as Porcupine Standing Sideways, a Shaman revered for his role in safeguarding his people from the Wendigo. Within these communities, the Wendigo was a very real threat. Over time, as hardships grew, so did the chance for Wendigo possession. Beliefs among some included ending the lives of those who had succumbed to its influence to eradicate Wendigo possession and stop its spread.

Zhauwuno-geezhigo-gaubow and his brother Pesequan were the sons of Peemeecheekag and would become known as Jack and Joseph Fiddler, respectively. Jack would take his father's place as a Shaman and leader of the Sucker clan. He also took up the mantle as protector against the Wendigo, alongside his brotherJoseph. In accordance with their beliefs, somewhere between 4 and 20 people's lives were ended to stop Wendigo possession.

In 1907, authorities external to the Clan (the Northwest Mounted Police) were alerted that a woman, Wahsakapeequay (Joseph's daughter-in-law), had been brought to the brothers for potential Wendigo possession. She was in excruciating pain, and to both ease her suffering and prevent her transformation to a Wendigo, the brothers ended her life through strangulation. The authorities arrested the brothers on June 15 for her death. Jack and Joseph offered to teach their clans a different way if the authorities were lenient, but the trial went on. And it became a newspaper sensation and a moral panic, with headlines like "Devil Worship Among the Cree."

Jack escaped after 15 weeks of captivity, then took his life in the woods. His brother Joseph's trial proceeded, though he had no legal representation. The Canadian Department of Justice had advised Joseph that such action was unnecessary. Though petitions emerged arguing Joseph had acted out of mercy and deserved the same in return, Joseph was sentenced to hang. While imprisoned at Stony Mountain Penitentiary, he contracted consumption. On September 4, 1909, an order for his release was issued — but it came too late. Joseph passed away just three days before the order arrived.

In 1907, Jack's son Robert became leader of the Sucker Clan. He signed Treaty 5, resulting in the five clans of the Sandy Lake area becoming the Deer Lake Band. Upon signing the treaty, Robert Fiddler became Chief by-election under the Indian Act for all five clans. Today, most of the descendants of Jack Fiddler live in the Sandy Lake First Nation, with others at the Deer Lake First Nation, and the North Spirit Lake First Nation in Ontario, and the three reserves at Island Lake in Manitoba.

Select Sources

Bissell, T. (2016, April 24). MEET JACK THE CANNIBAL KILLER. Ozy.

Bodine, T. (2019, October). The Wendigo Is Not Yours for the Taking. Ko-fi._https://ko-fi.com/post/The-Wendigo-Is-Not-Yours-for-the-Taking-C0C116U8P

Ferris, K. (2019, March 21). Zhauwuno-geezhigo-gaubow (Jack Fiddler) The Wendigo Killer. Dibaajimowin.

The First Hanging. (2011). Edmonton Journal.

Lewis, C., & Nelson, K. L. (2020). Wendigo Lore. On the Road Publications.

Peña, D. R. (2011, March). The Power to Punish: Conflicts of Authority in the Case of Jack Fiddler. Hypocrite Reader. http://www.hypocritereader.com/2/the-power-to-punish

Pitt, S. (2018, March 8). Windigo. The Canadian Encyclopedia.

SANDY LAKE FIRST NATION Treaty No. 5. (2021). SANDY LAKE FIRST NATION Treaty No. 5. http://www.sandylake.firstnation.ca/?q=history

Stevens, J. R. (2021). ZHAUWUNO-GEEZHIGO-GAUBOW. Dictionary of Canadian Biography. <http://www.biographi.ca/en/bio/zhauwuno_geezhigo_gaubow_13E.html>

Storm Walker, J. (n.d.). Swift Runner. God-and-Monsters.com. https://www.gods-and-monsters.com/swift-runner.html

Windigo: The Flesh-Eating Monster of Native American Legend | Monstrum. (n.d.). YouTube. <https://youtu.be/guiuXIMZ2vE?si=Ueu_8xZKUF---co1>

Salt

Season 1, Episode 3

Title: Dead in the Water

Dropped: December 10, 2020

In this episode,, we learn that to get rid of ghosts,, you need to "Find the remains, salt them, and burn them into dust," which made me curious about why salt is used in all the supernatural shows and movies to get rid of ghosts.

Salt. Humans love it. Deer love it. Ghosts hate it. Or do they? Besides in entertainment, where has salt been used to banish evil?

"Salt can be used to ward off demons. Salt is anti- demonic because it is a preservative and demons are creatures which are corrupt and destroy anything which has preservative qualities is contrary to their nature and they don't like it", according to '*The Black Arts*' by Richard Cavendish (Cavendish, 1983). Guess ghosts don't have my chip addiction.

Witchipedia.com says, "Salt may be used to create magical barriers against unwelcome entities. Standing within a circle of salt shields one from attack by these spirits, and sprinkling a line of salt on windowsills and doorways prevents then entering the home. Salt is said to absorb energy. To absorb negative energy in an area, sprinkle salt around the room, then sweep it up and discard it." You know you will be finding salt on your floor forever.

Things about salt can also get spicy. "Salted water represents life (salt itself symbolized semen," as is said in the Symbolic Significance of Salt by Ernest Jones. The dick association doesn't end there either. In Budge's *'Egyptian Ideas of the Future Life,'* salt is associated with a phallus, also a warder-off of evil, within the Egyptian Aphrodite mysteries (Budge, 2008). So dicks can be used to ward off evil instead of just causing it?

Speaking of dicks, salt has been used to improve sex lives since at least 1157. The French engraving *'Women Salting their Husbands'* shows four women holding down a man, pulling down his pants, and salting his behind for virility. There is an accompanying poem, perhaps a spell?

Kurlnasky notes that salt is the only way to break a zombie spell in Haiti. In parts of Africa and the Caribbean, some believe evil spirits disguised as women shed their skin at night and travel in the dark as balls of fire. To destroy these spirits, you must find their skin and salt it so they cannot return to it in the morning. (Kurlnasky, 2003).

Select Sources

Bourke, J. C. (2009). *Scatalogic Rites of All Nations.*

Buckland, R. (2002). *Buckland's Complete Book of Witchcraft.* Llewellyn Publications.

Budge, E.A. (2008). *Egyptian Ideas of the Future Life.* BiblioBazaar.

Cavendish, R. (1983). *The Black Arts: A Concise History of Witchcraft, Demonology, Astrology, and Other Mystical Practices Throughout the Ages.* TarcherPerigee.
de Givry, G. (1954).

Witchcraft, Magic and Alchemy.
Kurlnasky, M. (2003). *Salt: A World History.* Penguin Books.

Devils of Loudun

Season 1, Episode 4

Title: Phantom Traveler

Dropped: December 17, 2020

I chose this subject because it is one of the most famous documented cases of mass possession and exorcisms: The Devils of Loudun, or as I'm calling it, "Yoga Nuns." It has become one of my favorite examples of exorcisms as a tourist attraction.

Political Turmoil - Loudun, France, 1600s
In early 17th-century France, battles over religion raged between Catholics and Protestants (the Huguenots), the monarchy sought absolute rule, and, of course, every town still had its own internal struggles. One such town was Loudun, where two families, the Trincants and Brous, were embroiled in a feud for influence and control, and priests and nuns would soon turn the town upside down.

Urbain Grandier: F-boy Priest

In 1617, Loudun's parish church, Saint-Pierre-du-Marche (St. Peter of the Market), received a new priest, 27-year-old Urbain Grandier. Grandier's background seemed respectable and bourgeois enough for medieval France: his father was a lawyer, and his uncle a prominent Jesuit priest. He was charming and eloquent, and had no trouble finding women eager to help him break his vow of celibacy. He arrived in Loudun to find the town caught up in the aforementioned political turmoil and jumped right in.

At first, Grandier was well-liked in Loudun, even by some Huguenots. He made friends with the fashionable set and got along with both the Trincants and the Brous. Unfortunately, not everyone extended such a warm welcome to Grandier. Rene Le Mousnier, once the parish's junior priest, had been dismissed from his position due to a minor scandal. After his dismissal, Renes violently attacked an elderly priest, who also happened to be a friend of Grandier. After this attack, on Sunday, Grandier called out Rene, who happened to be watching from the back, for beating up an old man. Instead of showing remorse, Rene ran up to the pulpit and smacked Grandier. Full on Will Smithed. Grandier, of course, wasn't going to stand for that and proceeded to beat the crap out of Rene... still in the church! A few days later, at another mass, one of Rene's cousins tried to avenge Rene's humiliation by swinging on Grandier, but once again, Grandier whooped some church ass. I bet there were no problems getting anyone to attend mass that week. Then by some strange coincidence, a few days later, when Rene was returning to his village, he was attacked by 'random brigands,' and I believe murdered.

For almost a dozen years, Grandier maintained his popularity with his sharp wit and charm. He openly defied the elite, continued to get in physical altercations, and if he lost those, he often emerged victorious in legal battles. However, this period of luck could not last forever. As is want to happen when you have a lot of sex in a time before reliable birth control has been invented, Grandier's frolicking with the town's women resulted in pregnancies, including the daughter of his former friend and ally, **Trincant**. For revenge, Tricant told Grandier's bishop that Grandier was banging women in the church! As a result, the church tried and found Grandier guilty of immorality. The punishment for this crime was supposed to include the removal of him and his family from Loudun, as well as Grandier refraining from performing priestly duties for five years. Instead, the Governor intervened on Grandier's behalf, and together, they restored Grandier to his former position, although his reputation and likability were severely tarnished.

The Nuns: The Ursulines

In 1626, the Ursuline order established a new convent in Loudun, to the town's benefit. Finally, there was a place for girls to attend school. At the convent, young women could learn religion and prayers. If lucky, they might also be taught reading, writing, and basic arithmetic, along with skills like sewing, weaving, and lace-making—all considered appropriate for securing employment befitting "young ladies." In 1632, the Loudun convent had grown to 17 nuns from its initial 8. The nuns were approximately 25 years old on average, and they were led by the then 30-year-old Jeanne des Anges.

Jeanne des Anges - Sexy Hunchback
Jeanne des Anges cried her way into the world in the year 1602. A bout of tuberculosis early in life stunted her growth and left her with a hunchback. Regardless, she was still described as pretty, and her personality and spitefulness were cited as reasons she couldn't secure a good marriage. Whatever the reason, she did not find a husband, and instead, her dowry money went to the Ursulines when she became a nun.

When news came of a new convent opening in Loudun, Jeanne suddenly developed a much more agreeable persona, endearing herself to the aging prioress. When the prioress decided to retire, she recommended that Jeanne take over.

Meet Cute

When Jeanne met Grandier, she, like so many others, fell under his spell and developed an instant obsession for him, which continued for the next few years. Sadly for Jeanne, Grandier did not reciprocate her attraction, and to make things more awkward, Jeanne had offered Grandier a position as Director of the Convent, which he turned down, stating he was "too busy with my parish," and Jeanne, now rebuked twice, added Grandier to her enemy list. Perhaps out of spite, she appointed another of Grandier's rivals, Canon Mignon, to the position. Father Mignon, known for his jealousy towards Grandier, had also spent many years serving as the confessor to the convent nuns.

The Plague

In 1632, the people of Loudun were on edge, waiting for the plague that had ravaged their neighboring towns to come for them. They did their best to prepare. They established a hospital to put the sick outside the walls. They also appointed men to collect and bury the dead. These men would come through town ringing bells, sporting pointed, herb-filled masks, and wearing black robes marked with a cross on both the front and back. None of these things would stop the plague from killing about a quarter of the town's population, but at least they probably looked terrifying. The convent closed the school and locked its doors until the plague ran its terrible course. Now, it could be said there was already a lack of things to do in medieval times while hiding from a pandemic. After all, even books were still rare, and you can only play so many rounds of charades[2]. But cut off contact with the outside world, and things can get a little wild.

Sex Demons

The nuns of the convent began reporting shadow men walking the halls. These shadows, according to the nuns, were incubi (aka SEX DEMONS) sent by Satan under the direction of none other than Urbain Grandier. Jeanne said that Grandier was visiting her in her dreams, looking like a "radiant angel" but speaking like a devil, enticing her to acts of sex and vice. Perhaps under Jeanne's

---

2 Charades is thought to have been invented in France sometime in the 18th century. So maybe they weren't playing that, it just seemed more fun than talking about how much praying they were likely doing.

influence, or perhaps out of sheer boredom, the other nuns in the convent also began to talk about how local clergymen visited them for sexy times in their dreams, too.

To counteract the dreams and demons, Jeanne began a series of self-flagellation and penance. Loud penance. Loud enough that the convent was starting to get disturbed, and Father Mignon sprang into action.

He determined that the sex demons had possessed Jeanne and the other nuns. Father Mignon and his aide, Father Pierre Barre, exorcized the nuns who responded in fits and screams.

These nuns demonstrated their possession through the following physical anomalies:

- Shaking their heads up and down against their chests and back super fast
- Twisting around their arms at the joints of the shoulder, the elbow, and the wrist multiple times
- While on their stomachs, they joined the palms of their hands to the soles of their feet
- They lay themselves back till their heads

touched their feet, and walked in this position rapidly, and for a long time (eeww demon crab walk)

- While comatose, you could bend them into any shape, and they would stay that way
- Doing a straddle split (*I have been working on this for years. I may summon an incubus.*)
- Though only four feet tall, Jeanne managed to stretch toe to toe a distance of seven feet.

Though the women's physical agility was notable, several physicians who observed the exorcisms were skeptical that demons were the cause of their ability to master bow pose, and diagnosed the nuns as suffering from *furor uterinus - an agitated uterus known to quack doctors to make women insane and sick.*

Jeanne insisted that it was not her uterus making her so bendy, but in fact, it was the two demons Grandier put inside her:

Asmodeus and Zabulon. Asmodeus[3] is most commonly known as the Demon of Lust. In addition to lustiness, he hates marriage, and his chief reasons for being include wrecking new marriages, forcing husbands to commit adultery, and preventing husbands and wives from getting to do it. These all seem like married people needed a demon to blame for their problems. Usually portrayed as having three heads (an ogre, a ram, and a bull), the feet of a cock (rooster you perv), and wings and the tail of a serpent, he also rides on a dragon and breathes fire.

Not taking the accusation of controlling demons lightly, Grandier appealed his accusation to the Archbishop of Bordeaux, who sent his doctor to examine the nuns. The doctor saw no signs of possession but ordered the nuns to their rooms.

Things calmed for a bit, but maybe it was just too quiet, because Jeanne appeared in the convent yard in only a shirt and a rope around her neck. She then proceeded to stand in the

[3] The majority of the demon descriptions come from either Rosemary Ellen Guiley's The Encyclopedia of Demonology or M. Belanger's The Dictionary of Demons.

rain for two hours, tied herself to a tree, and threatened to hang herself. She complained that a third demon had arisen within her. This time, it was Iscaaaron, the devil of debauchery and blind lust, who causes people to have licentious thoughts. A lot of demons seem to focus on this lust thing. Iscaaaron appears as a three-legged dog, abhors pain, is blind to reason, and is violently passionate, although I am not sure about what.

Cardinal Richelieu sent his personal physician, Pilet de la Mesnardiere, who used his doctor skills to find out which demons were possessing these nuns and also WHERE in their bodies these possessions occurred:

- Jeanne
    - Leviathan was in the center of the forehead, Beherit in her stomach, Balaam under the second rib of the right side, and Isacaaron under the last rib on the left.
        - **Leviathan** is the demon of envy and faith. She is an aquatic, Arch-SHE-demon. Her breath is so foul that if you breathe it, you'll die.

- **Beherit** is a Duke. He commands 26 legions of demons and dresses like a soldier in a red uniform, wearing a gold crown and riding a red horse. If you summon him and ask him questions, he will speak honestly about the past, present, and future, but at any other time he speaks, he is lying. He can also turn metal into gold.

- **Balaam** is the demon of avarice, greed, and immorality. He is also a duke and commands 30 legions of demons. He has three heads: a bull, a man, and a ram. At least he doesn't have an ogre head like Asmodeus, that sounds hideous. He also has the tail of a snake's tail and flaming eyes. He speaks with a hoarse voice and rides a bear, carrying a goshawk on his wrist. A goshawk is a type of raptor.

- Sister Agnes
    - **Asmodeus** under the heart and **Beherit** in the stomach
- Louise of Jesus
    - **Eazaz** under the heart and **Caron** in the center of her forehead
- Claire de Sazilly:
    - **Zabulon** in the forehead, **Nepthali** in the right arm, **San Fin** under the 2nd rib on the right, **Elymi** on one side of the stomach, **Verrine** in the left temple, and **Concupiscence** of the order of the Cherubim in the left rib
- Seraphica
    - The stomach was bewitched, consisting of one drop of water, sometimes guarded by **Baruch** or **Carreau** (the demon of mercilessness who causes people to harden their hearts). I have no idea what that means.
- Anne d'Escoubleau
    - She had a magic bayberry leaf in her stomach guarded by Elymi.

- Non-nuns
  - Elizabeth Blanchard
    - Elizabeth had a devil under each armpit, the Coal of Impurity in the left buttock, and devils under the navel, below the heart, and under the left breast nipple.
  - Francoise Filatreau
    - Ginnillion in the forebrain, Jabel throughout the body, Buffetison below the navel, and Dog's Tail of the Order of Archangels in the stomach

After these examinations, the situation escalated even further. A Satanic panic began to spread, and men in Loudun were accused of consorting with the devil, the chief magistrate was accused of practicing black magic, and priests were accused of rape. Grandier was commanded to exorcise the demons, but he failed. He was put back on trial in 1634.

Grandier's 1634 Trial

During the trial, Jeanne allegedly vomited up a pact between the devil and Grandier, said to be stolen from Lucifer's cabinet of devilish agreements by Asmodeus. It was presented to the court as proof of Grandier's guilt. The pact was written in backward Latin and signed in blood. It detailed the costs and rewards for Grandier and was co-signed by Satan, Beelzebub, Lucifer, Elmi, Leviathan, and Astaroth. It was NOTARIZED by "signature and mark of the chief devil, and my lords the princes of hell." The recorder, Baalberith, countersigned the pact. Asmodeus also wrote out a promise to leave one of the nuns he was possessing." This was a real thing that still exists and, I believe, is available for viewing at the Bibliothèque Nationale in France.

Trigger warning: may induce vomiting

The following were also vomited up during this trial: eight orange seeds, a bundle of five straws, and a package containing worms, cinders, hair, and nail clippings.

Jeanne additionally threw up a pact which was said to include a piece of the heart of a child who had been sacrificed in 1631 at a witches' sabbath near Orleans, the ashes of a eucharist, and some of Grandier's blood and semen. This court was full of biohazards.

Grandier's testimony for this trial was all gathered during extensive torture, including the application of a Spanish boot—an iron casing for his legs—resulting in the breaking of both. This may have weighed on Jeanne's conscience, and she tried to retract her testimony dramatically, in a way only she could. She arrived in court with a noose wrapped around her neck and threatened to end her life if she couldn't take it all back.

Her pleadings were to no avail, and Grandier was sentenced to death by burning on August 18, 1634. He was given the opportunity for a final statement and an option for strangulation before the flames, but neither occurred. Instead, he was led to the stake by friars who doused him in Holy Water to silence him, and then burned him alive. A witness reported that a large fly, likely Beelzebub, buzzed around his head as he perished.

Ursuline Convent Post-Grandier

After Grandier's execution, the exorcisms of the nuns continued. These exorcisms had become something of a tourist attraction and now took place twice a day on a schedule for the public to observe. Maybe adding to the draw was that the nuns would lift their skirts while begging for sex during these exorcisms. They still did all the previously mentioned contortions while, in general, being lewd and not very nun-like. New Jesuit priests arrived, including Father Jean-Joseph Surin, whose arrival caused Jeanne to go into fits, howl, and run away while sticking out her tongue.

Jeanne developed a false pregnancy; her stomach distended, she stopped menstruating, and she secreted breast milk. The pregnancy ended when Isacaaron arose at an exorcism, declaring it was all his deception.

It was all the rage at the time to become a Saint, so Jeanne set her mind to becoming venerated. A woman of action, she increased her prayer time, started wearing a hair shirt, slept on a board of nails, put wormwood in her food, and got a belt made of spiked nails (punk AF Jeanne). These efforts impressed Father Surin, who began having private sessions with Jeanne.

Father Jean-Joseph Surin

In October 1635, Father Surin was ordered by the Church to return to Bordeaux, and a new exorcist took his place. While he was away, Jeanne fell ill and begged Surin to come back. Upon Surin's return, he expelled Leviathan from Jeanne in front of a crowd. A bloody cross appeared on Jeanne's forehead, lasting for three weeks. Following additional exorcisms, her arm bore the names of Joseph, Jesus, Mary, and St. Francis de Sales. Although these names faded after a few weeks, they were mysteriously renewed by Jeanne's "angel." Surin ultimately departed after failing to exorcise the demon Behemoth from Jeanne over a span of ten months.

Miracles, Demons, and Royalty

A new priest, Father Resses, came and performed more exorcisms on Jeanne. This time vomited blood, and was so sick she was given Last Rites. But while on her deathbed, she had a vision of an angel and St. Joseph, who anointed her with oil, and she miraculously recovered. She later showed her chemise had an oil stain of five drops, and it became a holy relic.

She still hadn't quite gotten rid of all her demons, and the demon Behemoth told Jeanne that for him to leave, she had to go on a pilgrimage to the tomb of St Francis of Sales at Annecy, and additionally, Father Surin had to go with her. Her journey lasted five months, and Father Surin accompanied her for part of it. She went through Paris, Lyon, and numerous other towns. Again, since there wasn't much to do in a medieval village, tens of thousands came to witness her miraculous arm and chemise. She met with the then-dying Cardinal Richelieu and even had her oily chemise used as a blanket during the birth of Louis XIV. All of this travel seemed to work, and the demon Behemoth was expelled. Surin returned to Bordeaux, and Jeanne to Loudun for good this time.

The End of Jeanne and Surin

The town of Loudun continued to be a hot spot for exorcisms until 1637, when Cardinal Richelieu withdrew church funding. Jeanne suffered from an extreme lack of attention, but nobody cared. She fell ill and miraculously recovered. Nobody cared. She began to write her autobiography in 1644, in which she documented her life as a "spiritual quest, in which she had allowed demons to act against her as a consequence of her own defective will."

She continued to write to Father Surin, who ignored her until 1657, when he resumed being her spiritual advisor until his death. Before this death, Surin tried to kill himself by jumping out of a second-floor window, said to have inspired the scene at the end of The Exorcist. Only Surin survived and remained massively depressed.

The tides also turned against Jeanne, who was branded a witch and magician by her detractors until her death in January 1665. Following her execution, her severed head was placed in a silver and gold reliquary, while her stained chemise was kept separately. Both items became objects of popular devotion. The convent also commissioned a grand painting depicting Jeanne and the expulsion of Behemoth, which hung within its walls for 80 years until a Bishop ordered its removal. Not going without a fight, the nuns concealed the painting by covering it with another. However, in 1772, the convent was closed, and the painting, chemise, and head were hidden away and eventually disappeared, never to be seen again.

Select Sources

Bane, Theresa. Encyclopedia of Demons in World Religions and Cultures. McFarland, 2012.

Guiley, Rosemary Ellen. The Encyclopedia of Demons & Demonology. Facts On File, 2009.

Infographic Show. "The Demonic Possession Of The Nuns Of Loudun." YouTube.

Laycock, Dr. Joseph, editor. The Penguin Book of Exorcisms. Penguin Classics, 2020.

Rapley, Robert. A Case of Witchcraft: The Trial of Urbain Grandier. McGill-Queen's University Press, 1998.

"Eastern Air Lines Flight 401." Wikipedia, Wikimedia Foundation. https://en.wikipedia.org/wiki/Eastern_Air_Lines_Flight_401.

"Exorcism." Supernatural Wiki. http://www.supernaturalwiki.com/Exorcism.

"Father Urbain Grandier Sold His Soul to the Devil—and You Can See the Contract Right Here!" Week in Weird, 23 Nov. 2016. http://weekinweird.com/2016/11/23/father-urbain-grandier-sold-his-soul-to-the-devil-and-you-can-see-the-contract-right-here/.

"A Jesuit Mystic's Feminine Melancholia: Jean Joseph." Questia. https://www.questia.com/library/journal/1G1-189052346/a-jesuit-mystic-s-feminine-melancholia-jean-joseph.

"The Number 40 in the Bible." Numerology Center. http://numerology.center/biblical_numbers_number_40.php.

"Urbain Grandier." Wikipedia, Wikimedia Foundation. https://en.wikipedia.org/wiki/Urbain_Grandier.

"Zabulon, the Lord of Hell." Vimeo. https://vimeo.com/14581423.

Bloody Mary and Whitewater, Wisconsin (The Second Salem)

Season 1, Episode 5

Title: Bloody Mary

Dropped: November 11, 2021

Sometimes you just go where the lore takes you, and the Bloody Mary lore took me to Whitewater, Wisconsin. A version of this was published in the Austin Seance Journal in 2025.

If you were an American girl at a slumber party within the past fifty years, you probably played or were dared to play Bloody Mary. This is when you would stand in front of a mirror (usually with some kind of flashlight or candle because of course, the lights are off) and say "Bloody Mary" or something similar, like "I stole your baby Bloody Mary," a certain number of times, and then her spirit would appear in the mirror, maybe claw your eyes or something. While versions of this seem to go back forever, it appears that folklorists didn't start writing about the 'Bloody Mary Game' until the 1960s/70s. Some have posited that it is a metaphor for the onset of a girl's period.

The Italian Psychologist Giovanni Caputo conducted an experiment in which observers were seated in a dim room in front of a mirror and told to stare at their reflection. Over 66 percent of participants perceived significant deformations in their own faces, a phenomenon known as the "Strange Face Illusion." This could account for seeing something spooky in a mirror in a dimly lit room.

But what about the woman, Bloody Mary, herself? Three women are usually brought as possible contenders as inspiration: Queen Mary I, responsible for the deaths of hundreds by fire; Countess Elizabeth Bathory, who, as a fun fact, did NOT bathe in the blood of virgins to stay young; or sometimes Mary Worth, a Wisconsin witch, who may or may not have existed. Plenty has been written about the first two, so let's discuss Mary Worth.

Now, the first question I hear you asking: witches in Wisconsin? And I have to put on my

Hermione hat and say, "Well, actually, there is a town, Whitewater, Wisconsin, that bills itself as the Second Salem."

Whitewater, Wisconsin

Today, Whitewater, Wisconsin, is home to the University of Wisconsin-Whitewater and has a population of about 15,000 people. The name came from the Potawatomi Native Americans who settled along the Whitewater River after being displaced by the Beaver Wars. I will keep my juvenile comments about the Beaver Wars to myself. The name Wau-be-gan-naw-po-cat, meaning "white water," was given because of the white sand in the water.

White settlement of the town began in 1836, when Alvin Foster staked his claim by marking his name on a tree. Seriously, that is all you had to do. It was legal. The next year, Samuel Prince built the first log cabin near the current site of "Whitewater's Indian Mounds Park" (also known as Whitewater Effigy Mounds Preserve). It is believed that this area was once settled by the Potawatomi people,, who had at least 30 circular huts there. Within the park, you can find 12 or 13 effigy mounds near Whitewater Creek.

The town grew in the 1840s, gaining streets, stores, hotels, and a few dozen homes. Industrialism came to town between 1850 and 1888. Esterly Reaper Works began manufacturing mechanical harvesting machines and other farm equipment, soon becoming the largest employer in the 1880s, with 525 employees. Esterly employees built homes close to the factory on the east side of the city, and the surrounding area became known as "Reaperville".

Spiritualism and Whitewater
The Spiritualist movement began spreading across the country in the late 1840s, and the Whitewater area soon developed an active Spiritualist community, including the territory's third appointed governor, Nathaniel P. Tallmadge, who claimed his daughter had been taught to play piano by spirits. Spirit knocking, channeling, healing, and automatic writings were occurring all over Wisconsin. Seances in the homes within the Lake Mills area attracted renowned mediums from

around the country, including Cora Scott Richmond and Victoria Woodhull. At one of these, New York transplant Morris Pratt, who moved to the area in the 1850s, is introduced to the psychic healer Mary Hayes-Chynoweth.

Mary, the child of a Free Will Baptist minister, came to Wisconsin as a girl. She married Anson Hayes, a cousin of President Rutherford B. Hayes, and together they had three children; two made it to adulthood. Mary was a known healer and traveled around Wisconsin, curing people by taking on their sickness herself. Mary, at times, could converse with the sick in their native tongues, even those unbeknownst to her. She took no money for healing. Mary became friends with Warren Chase, a Spiritualist who published a weekly paper called the "Spiritualist Telegraph - Devoted to the Illustration of Spiritual Intercourse." Chase encouraged her to start attending the seances at Lake Mills; however, she was not a medium in the sense that she was not channeling spirits at these seances.

When Morris and Mary met, he was a moderately successful farmer. Mary hears him say that if he had real money, he would dedicate much of it to the study of Spiritualism. Mary tells him about this investment opportunity she learned about from her "controlling spirit," an old German professor, if he wants to put his money where his mouth is. She says that if he invests with her sons in this area of land in Northern Wisconsin, she will promise him a return. He invested with her sons, who opened the Ashland iron mine and proceeded to dig. A couple of years pass with no return; however, in 1886, the miners discover the Gogebic iron range, one of the largest iron ranges in the region, and Pratt becomes wealthy overnight. Pratt would keep his word and begin construction on the corner of Center and Third Streets in Whitewater in 1888. Pratt designed the building as a temple and a school for Spiritualism. Pratt and his wife, Mary Jane, took one apartment, and there was a second guest apartment. Two more floors housed two lecture halls (one of which seated nearly 400 people), 12 dormitory rooms, and offices. There was also a rumored seance room on the third floor, painted entirely white, which only select Spiritualists were allowed to enter.

The locals laughed and called it "Pratt's Folly." Their affection was not gained when, during the 1889 dedication, an Indiana Spiritualist gave a sermon ridiculing other religions, outraging the town. This didn't seem to affect Pratt, who focused on making the temple a place for the Study of Spiritualism, including regular Sunday services, seances, classes, and lectures. Spiritualists from all over came to stay in the dorms, further annoying the town, which added "Spook's Temple" to its nickname.

In 1901, he filed for the incorporation of the Morris Pratt Institution Association, a school whose curriculum would include Comparative Theology and Psychic Culture. The subjects taught would be Science, Mathematics, Language, Oratory, Voice and Physical Culture, English and Rhetoric, Bible Exegetics, Higher Criticism, Logic and Parliamentary Law, Comparative Theology, and Psychic Culture. It would attract only a dozen students.

In December 1902, Morris Pratt transitioned, but the Institute lived on. It is a legend that who Pratt deeded the building to is unknown, but I suspect it was the seven Trustees: Moses Hull, A. J. Weaver, J. C. Bump, W. H. Rogers, Clara L. Stewart, Alonzo Thompson, and C. L. Stevens.

The institute sold the building in 1946. The new owners briefly opened it as a rest home for aged Spiritualists. Later, it was used as a girls' dormitory for the nearby Wisconsin Teachers' College. It was torn down in 1961 and replaced by a new office for the Wisconsin Telephone Company. After selling the building in Whitewater, the school moved to Milwaukee, where it still exists today, remaining one of the few places in the world dedicated to the study of telepathy, clairvoyance, mediumship, and psychic surgery.

So, who was Bloody Mary Worth?
In the 1890s, a depression settled over the town when factories, including the Winchester and Partridge Wagon works, closed, putting hundreds of men out of work. One of these

was owned by the Wincester family, and the Whitewater Chamber of Commerce Tour claims a witch named Mary Worth may have cursed the Winchesters. Three members of the family died within a year plus the family's business was shut down. According to the legend, the cemetery board decided against burying her in the hallowed ground of of Hillside Cemetery, instead placing her in an above-ground crypt, resulting in all of Whitewater being cursed. To this date, they haven't found any records verifying any of this, including Mary Worth's existence. But you can hear all about her in one of the town's many ghost tours.

Select Sources

"1.05 Bloody Mary." Supernatural Wiki. http://www.supernaturalwiki.com/1.05_Bloody_Mary.

"Aztalan State Park." Wisconsin Historical Society. https://www.wisconsinhistory.org/Records/Article/CS309.

Barnard, K. A. "Postmortem Hemorrhage." Barnard Health. https://www.barnardhealth.us/forensic-pathology/postmortem-hemorrhage.html.

"Bloody Mary Legend." HowStuffWorks. https://people.howstuffworks.com/bloody-mary-legend.htm.

"Bloody Mary Story." Snopes. https://www.snopes.com/fact-check/bloody-mary-story/.

"Bloody Mary." Jesterbear. http://www.jesterbear.com/Wicca/BloodyMary2.html.

Caputo, Giovanni B. "Strange-face-in-the-mirror illusion." Perception 39 (2010): 1007-1008.

"History of Whitewater." Discover Whitewater. https://www.discoverwhitewater.org/tourism-council/history-of-whitewater.

Herhold, John. "Herhold: The woman behind San Jose's Hayes Mansion." Mercury News. June 14, 2016. https://www.mercurynews.com/2016/06/14/herhold-the-woman-behind-san-joses-hayes-mansion/.

Higgypop. "Spirit Cabinets." Higgypop. https://www.higgypop.com/news/spirit-cabinets/.

Hirst, Arlene. "Bloody Mary in the Mirror." LiveAbout. Updated October 18, 2020. https://www.liveabout.com/bloody-mary-in-the-mirror-3299478.

"Indian Mounds Park (Whitewater, Wisconsin)." Wikipedia. \[[suspicious link removed]\>.

Morris Pratt Institute. http://www.morrispratt.org/.

"Morris Pratt Institute Builder." Spiritual Path Spiritualist Church. https://www.spiritualpathspiritualistchurch.org/morris-pratt-institute-builder/.

"Morris Pratt Institute of Spiritualism." Cult of Weird. https://www.cultofweird.com/paranormal/morris-pratt-institute-of-spiritualism/.

"Morris Pratt Institute of Spiritualism." Cult of Weird. https://www.cultofweird.com/paranormal/morris-pratt-institute-of-spiritualism/.

"Spirit Tour." Whitewater Chamber. https://www.whitewaterchamber.com/spirit-tour/.

"Spiritual Telegraph." IAPSOP. http://iapsop.com/archive/materials/spiritual_telegraph/.

"Spiritualism." Wikipedia. https://en.wikipedia.org/wiki/Spiritualism.

"Strangers in the Mirror." Haunted Auckland. https://hauntedauckland.com/site/strangers-in-the-mirror/.

"The Esterly Reaper." Hoard Museum. https://hoardmuseum.org/esterly-reaper/.

"The strange face in the mirror illusion." MindHacks. September 18, 2010. https://mindhacks.com/2010/09/18/the-strange-face-in-the-mirror-illusion/.

"Top 5 Haunted Places in Whitewater, WI aka The Second Salem." Discover Whitewater. https://www.discoverwhitewater.org/blog/top-5-haunted-places-in-whitewater-wi-aka-the-second-salem.

"Vintage Wisconsin: World's first spiritualist school founded in Wisconsin." APG-WI. December 14, 2017. https://www.apg-wi.com/vintage-wisconsin-worlds-first-spiritualist-school-founded-in-wisconsin/article_f0e3547c-e117-11e7-a76b-0b615da76190.html.

Whitewater Historical Society. "Spiritualism: The Morris Pratt Institute." Whitewater Historical Society. https://www.whitewaterhistoricalsociety.org/post/spiritualism-the-morris-pratt-institute.

Wisconsin Historical Society. Wisconsin History. https://www.wisconsinhistory.org/Records/Article/CS2718.

Wisconsin Historical Society. Wisconsin History. https://www.wisconsinhistory.org/Records/Newspaper/BA12733.

Wisconsin Public Radio. "World's First Spiritualist School Founded in Wisconsin." WPR. https://www.wpr.org/education/worlds-first-spiritualist-school-founded-wisconsin.

"Wisconsin's Lost Towns." Wisconsin Historical Society. https://www.wisconsinhistory.org/Records/Article/CS301.

Witches of Whitewater Documentary. US Paranormal Research. https://

www.usparanormalresearch.com/witches-of-whitewater-documentary.html.

"Woodhull & Claflin's Weekly, V. 7, No. 19, April 11, 1874." IAPSOP. http://iapsop.com/archive/materials/woodhull_and_claflins_weekly/woodhull_and_claflins_weekly_v7_n19_apr_11_1874.pdf.

Wortman, Sharon. "Legends abound regarding Bloody Mary." Lake County Journal. October 14, 2013. https://www.lakecountyjournal.com/2013/10/14/legends-abound-regarding-bloody-mary-worth/ano8osd/.

"Why is it bad luck to break a mirror?" HowStuffWorks. https://people.howstuffworks.com/why-is-it-bad-luck-to-break-mirror.htm.

Doppelgangers

Season 1, Episode 6

Title: Skin

Dropped: November 18, 2021

The episode was called " Doppelganger, " so the subject matter directed itself. Surprisingly, my many watchings of Vampire Diaries did not help with the research at all.

The word doppelganger is German for 'double walker' or a 'double goer'. It has also been defined as a phenomenon of "a non-biologically related look-alike or double of a living person." So, in essence, a copy of a person. And it can be a ghost or just a weird thing.

Not surprisingly, seeing your doppelganger is considered a bad omen. The superstition is that you see yourself, and that means you're likely to get sick or die. To be clear, a doppelganger is not the same as your "dead ringer". If you see someone who looks like you but not exactly like you, you PROBABLY won't die (I don't know your risk profile). A doppelganger is more of a spiritual reflection of a person. The concept goes back at least as far as the ancient Egyptians, who believed in a *ka* or spirit double. In Norse mythology, the vardøger was a double who did everything their counterpart would do, but before it did. Confused? Me too. But as far as I understand it, they would see a person's double show up and do all their normal activities before the other person arrived. As an introvert and self-proclaimed hermit, that sounds like a heavenly notion. I don't have to go to a party and make small talk? Will my vardøger do it for me? Sold.

There is a long history of famous people seeing their doppelgangers. Just to name drop a few: Goethe, Queen Elizabeth I, and Percy Shelley. One of the most famous accounts was of Abraham Lincoln, who said he saw his doppelganger more than once. On the more spooky side, he apparently saw a double version of himself in a mirror, and Mary Todd predicted based on that he wouldn't live to see a second term in office.

My favorite historical account was the one about Catherine the Great's doppelganger. One night, she was lying in what I imagine was a killer bed, when her servants ran in and told her they had JUST seen her enter the throne room. Clearly, she had to see what was going on, and when she entered the throne room, she saw herself sitting on her throne. Being the woman she was, she ordered her team to shoot her. The stories don't tell whether the bullet had any effect on whoever or whatever was sitting on the throne, but the real Catherine died soon afterward.

Emilie Sagee

One of the most written about doppelganger cases is that of Emilie
Sagee. The author Robert Dale Owen first heard about Emilie Sagee through Julie von Güldenstubbe, the second daughter of Baron von Güldenstubbe. We do know that Julie von Güldenstubbe existed, as she and her brother were among the Spiritualist movement. Admit it, you're saying von Güldenstubbe out loud.

According to Julie, she attended a girls' school near modern-day Latvia in 1845, and there she met Emilie Sagee. Emilee was said to have been born in Dijon, France, in 1813. By the time she arrived at the school Pensionat von Neuwelcke, she had previously been employed at 18 different schools. But they were so desperate for teachers, they hired her. So Emilee starts teaching,, and everyone likes her at first. But then 13 of her students said they saw Emilee's doppelganger standing beside her, mirroring her movements as she wrote on a chalkboard. Of course, nobody believed this. Then, the students said they saw her doppelganger again while she was eating lunch, standing behind her, mimicking her movements.

Nearly 50 students witnessed the largest account. These students were in class sewing, with another teacher at the front reading a book, while Emilie was outside in the garden. When the teacher who had been sitting in the front left the room, the students saw Emilee come in and take a seat. Then the students looked out the window and saw the other Emilee still out in the garden! Some of the students went up and touched the doppelganger Emilee, and later recounted that she felt like cobwebs. Upon further questioning, the non-cobweb Emilee said, of course, she had been in the garden and didn't know what they were talking about, although at the time she had wished she had been in the classroom. Emilee never once admitted to having seen her shadow self, although anytime her double was seen, she became very tired, and whatever her other self did was something she was thinking about. Emilee and the second Emilee were seen many more times, and the parents started freaking out and removed their children from the school. Due to this, she was eventually fired.

Modern Thoughts?

People once thought that doppelgangers were demons. In today's enlightened times, some people think that doppelgangers are astral projecting or creating multiple versions of themselves in alternate time phases. Or maybe it's mental health, and people are hallucinating due to various causes like lack of sleep or schizophrenia.

Select Sources

"A Cultural History of the Doppelgänger." Atlas Obscura.\[https://www.atlasobscura.com/articles/history-doppelganger\]

"Doppelganger." Mythology.net.\[https://mythology.net/others/concepts/doppelganger/\]

"Doppelgänger." Wikipedia.\[https://en.wikipedia.org/wiki/Doppelg%C3%A4nger\]

"Émilie Sagée." Wikipedia.\[https://en.wikipedia.org/wiki/%C3%89milie_Sag%C3%A9e\]

"Johann Ludwig von Güldenstubbe." Wikipedia.\[https://de.wikipedia.org/wiki/Johann_Ludwig_von_G%C3%BCldenstubbe\]

"9 Mystifying Cases of the Doppelganger Phenomenon." The Martian Herald.\[https://www.martianherald.com/9-mystifying-cases-doppelganger-phenomenon/page/9\]

"The Curious Case of Émilie Sagée's Bilocation." The Curious Archive.\[https://www.curiousarchive.com/emilie-sagee-bilocation-doppelganger/\]

"The Time When You're Most Likely to See Your Doppelgänger." Vice.\[https://www.vice.com/en/article/the-time-when-you're-most-likely-to-see-your-doppelgnger/\]

"Twin Strangers Exist." Twin Strangers.\[https://twinstrangers.net/twin-strangers-exist\]

Urban Legends/Phantom Killer of Texarkana

Season 1, Episode 7

Title: Hook Man

Dropped: January 7, 2021

The monster of the week, "The Hook Man," is a combination of three urban legends, all centered mainly around the moral lesson that young people, or more specifically, girls, shouldn't get too wild, as they may face dire consequences, possibly even death. I came across the story of the Phantom Killer while researching "Lovers Lane Murders." Please destroy my search history upon my demise.

Don't Turn on The Light
The first urban legend is commonly called the "Don't Turn on the Light." Snopes.com tells it this way: a college girl enters her dorm room after a night out partying, she doesn't want to disturb her roommate, and so she doesn't turn on any lights. The following day, she awakes

to find her roommate murdered, and a note asking, "Aren't you glad you didn't turn on the light?" There are known variations of this back to at least 1871, including some extra horrific ones with a dead dog. In addition to trying to scare the youth into paying attention, some say this story also highlights the human fear of being vulnerable to random violence.

The Dead Boyfriend
The second legend is known as "The Dead Boyfriend." Again, according to Snopes, the legend goes: a girl is sitting in a car, waiting for her boyfriend to return with gasoline (hopefully not in a plastic bag[4]). While sitting there, she starts to hear an eerie screech or scrape. She doesn't leave the car until the police show up to rescue her. The police get the girl out of the car and tell her not to turn around, but she does anyway to see her dead boyfriend hanging from a tree over the car, his body making the scraping sound as the wind drags it back and forth.

____

[4] When I originally wrote this, people were freaking out about a gas storage and some were going to the gas stations with plastic bags. Don't do that.

The earliest documented version of this story was collected by the folklorist Daniel R. Barnes in 1964 from a freshman at the University of Kansas. This legend varies in structure by location, particularly by which side of the Atlantic it's told. In the American versions, the boyfriend dangles from a tree above the car, his fingernails scraping the roof. In Europe, the killer is there holding the boyfriend's head and tapping on the roof with an ax. But in both, the idea of not looking back is a central theme. What is the lesson here? If you go too far from home with a strange boy, someone will die. Or maybe never drive with less than a quarter tank in your car.

The Hook Man

The third urban legend is the episode's namesake, "The Hook Man." Once again from Snopes: this legend finds a young couple making out in a lover's lane when suddenly, on the radio, an emergency bulletin alerts of an escaped killer with a hook for a hand on the loose. The girl wants to go home and eventually convinces the guy to leave. When they get to her house, there is a bloody hook hanging from the door handle of the car. The moral of the story is: If you make out, you will die, or get really scared. An interesting perspective on this legend comes from an article written by Wolf Schweitzer in which he discusses why this type of violence so often associated with a prosthetic: "a missing hand, a stump, a prosthetic hook if not a prosthetic arm generally and very clearly indicate a perceived loss of humanity. ... With that, amputees (including "the hook" variety) are seen as if they remove themselves from the whole of society (regardless of the fact that society expels or rejects them to begin with), and that makes them unsafe as they are not part of what is assumed to be the safety of civilization."

Those three make up the urban legends from this episode. Are any of them based in reality? Several couples seeking privacy have been murdered while hidden in the shadows. These cases are often unsolved, likely due to the inherent difficulty of solving cases in which victims and perpetrators are unknown to each other, compared with those committed by acquaintances.

A few examples:

In 1930, Queens, New York, a man attacked two different couples in secluded areas, killing the men, assaulting the women, then sending the women to a bus stop with a letter for the press. He was never caught.

In 1968, David Arthur Faraday (17) and Betty Lou Jensen (16) were the first couple whose murder was attributed to the Zodiac Killer in Benicia, California. Those murders continued through at least 1969. The identity of the Zodiac Killer remains undetermined.

From 1986-1990, four couples were killed on Colonial Parkway in Virginia. Also, never solved.

In 1990, 22-year-old Cheryl Henry and 21-year-old Andy Atkinson were murdered in an isolated cul-de-sac in West Houston. A golf club and 3 golf balls were found pointing to Cheryl's body, about 200 yards from the car. Again, never solved, although there was a DNA match to a rape victim who was attacked two months before the murders.

Phantom Killer of Texarkana

The "Texas Moonlight Murders," also known as the Phantom Killer of Texarkana, were a series of killings straight out of an urban legend that happened in Texarkana, Texas, back in the 1940s.

Texarkana is often referred to as a single town. Still, technically, it's two towns situated right on the Texas-Arkansas border, each with its own government. Texarkana was settled mainly by those who wanted a place with little law enforcement. You know, criminals. And those outlaws enjoyed their good times. By 1888, Texarkana had 23 saloons! That rough-and-tumble life persisted for a long time, leaving its mark on the area. The red light district was around well past WWII. Violence and crime plagued the town, though many tried to change its image. In 1946, the year this crime occurred, the population was still relatively small. There were only about 52,000 people, both sides of the border included, and you could drive across town in a matter of minutes.

Jimmy Hollis and Mary Jeanne Larey

Jimmy Hollis (25) and Mary Jeanne Larey (19) were parking out at "lovers lane" after leaving a movie and having late-night snacks with friends on the way to Mary Jeanne's home in Hooks, Texas, in February 1946. While they were making out, a man approached the car and told Jimmy to get out and take off his pants. Ok, more like the man screamed at Jimmy to "take off your goddamned pants!" He complied, and his reward was to get pistol-whipped. The man told Mary Jeanne to run, and she also complied. Then he caught her and asked, "Why are you running?" He then sexually assaulted her with the pistol. Headlights approached, scaring off the attacker. Eventually, Mary was able to summon help, and they were taken to the hospital. They both survived but had different versions of who their attacker was, not unusual during traumatic situations. However, the police began to accuse Mary of lying about not knowing who attacked her, and she felt harassed enough that she left Texarkana.

Richard Griffin and Polly Ann Morre
On March 24, Richard Griffin and Polly Ann Morre went to a midnight movie and then to a cafe for snacks. I appreciate how late you could get snacks in this town back then. On their way home, they pulled off Bowie County Highway 67 for unknown reasons, and later their bodies were found in their car. Both were shot with a .32 caliber revolver; Richard's pants were around his ankles.

No attempt was made to preserve the crime scene. It seems that half of Texarkana came out and trampled the crime scene, which was already soggy from the rain. The large, unruly crowd included two drunk women who got in a fight and wrestled in the dirt. This was at least after the bodies and car had been moved. No suspect was identified, and this case was unrelated to what happened to Jimmy and Mary Jeane at the time.

Betty Jo Booker and Paul Martin
On April 14, 15-year-old Betty Jo Booker finished her gig playing saxophone with the local band, the Rhythmaires, at a VFW club.

She met up with her 17-year-old friend, Paul Martin, who was visiting from Kilgore, at 2 am. They were supposed to go meet up with some of Betty Jo's friends at a slumber party, but on the way, they stopped at Spring Lake. The two had not been romantically linked before, and it is highly likely they were just talking. Even if that was the case, Paul was found shot dead on the shoulder of the road. Betty Jo would be found two miles from Paul.

This couple's murder escalated tensions in the town, particularly because this couple was so young. To bolster the investigation, the Texas Ranger, Captain Manuel Trazazas "El Lobo Solo" Gonzaullas, was brought in from Dallas to lead the investigation and began holding press conferences at the downtown Grim Hotel. He was an impressive-looking man, described by the reporter Louis "Swampy" Graves as "wearing sharply creased whipcord trousers with a short jacket, boots with a high sheen, carrying pistols with ivory handles, all crowned with a Stetson." His pistols can be seen in the Texas Ranger Hall of Fame archive and are described as Colt Standard 1911s, 45-caliber, factory-engraved with gold inlay, cutaway trigger guards, gold monogrammed initials on the right, and a longhorn on the left of the ivory grips. Each pistol is inscribed near the trigger with the motto, "Never Draw Me Without Cause, Nor Shield Me With Dishonor."

Gonzaullus' questioned suspects and drew a distasteful opinion of Texarkana. He told the local editor, "Texarkana has more human driftwood than I've ever been in, other than San Antonio or El Paso. You have more petty thieves, more prostitutes, more pimps, more of an underworld than any big city."

When no murderer was found, traps were set to lure the killer or killers out. One I call the Bugs Bunny plan: A Ranger would drive out to a deserted road with a dressed-up female mannequin. Then the Ranger would pretend to make out with the mannequin. To be fair, I don't know if that part was true, but they surely tried to sell it. Other cops attempted a similar tactic. They would disguise themselves as couples parking, with one of the lawmen as a woman. I assume they also made out. Shockingly, this didn't work.

Texarkana's fears continued to rise. Gun stores as far away as Dallas ran out of guns. People asked for a curfew for teens. The midnight movie was canceled. With no definitive answers coming from law enforcement, the rumor mill began running full force, and untrue stories started circulating, like the girls had been mutilated, making things worse.

Virgil and Katy Starks

Things went quiet for about a month. On the night of May 3, Katy Starks was at home when she heard glass shatter downstairs. When she went to check on the noise, she found her husband, Virgil, fatally shot in the back of his head. She ran to the phone but, while trying to call for help, two more shots came in from the window, both hitting her face. Even with all of this, she kept her wits and crawled to the back of the house. Upon entering the kitchen, she saw the attacker throwing a leg through the window. She turned around and went the other way through the house. Escaping the front door, she ran across the street to her sister's house, who didn't answer her frantic knocks. She ran to the next house, and when the homeowner opened his door, he grabbed his gun and shot it in the air. Then the other neighbor came running over and offered his car. They piled into the car and drove Katy to the hospital. She survived the two shots to her face; however, whoever was in the house remained on the run and unknown.

This didn't make Texarkana any calmer, and the police were inundated with false reports, including the report of two dead bodies, which ended up being two cows that had successfully escaped their cattle truck, only to fall asleep in someone's yard. I don't know the outcome for the cows. I also can't tell you the definitive outcome for the Phantom Killer. They went through over a thousand suspects, but nobody was ever convicted. Two men remain at the top of most investigators' lists, but they have both died.

Select Sources

"10 Disturbing Facts About The Colonial Parkway Murders." Listverse. https://listverse.com/2018/06/25/10-disturbing-facts-about-the-colonial-parkway-murders/.

"Aren't You Glad You Didn't Turn on the Light?" Snopes. https://www.snopes.com/fact-check/arent-you-glad-you-didnt-turn-on-the-light/?collection-id=209633.

Brunvand, Jan Harold. "NEW LEGENDS FOR OLD." ETC: A Review of General Semantics 43, no. 4 (1986): 381-88. [suspicious link removed].

"Cheryl Henry & Andy Atkinson: Lovers Lane Murders Houston." True Crime Diva. https://truecrimediva.com/cheryl-henry-andy-atkinson-lovers-lane-murders-houston/.

"The Boyfriend's Death." Snopes. https://www.snopes.com/fact-check/the-boyfriends-death/.

"The Dead Boyfriend." LiveAbout. https://www.liveabout.com/the-dead-boyfriend-3299479.

"Episode 3: Cheryl Henry & Andy Atkinson." A Southern Sleuth Podcast, 2019. https://asouthernsleuthpodcast.com/2019/03/17/episode-3-cheryl-henry-andy-atkinson/.

"The Horrifying Texarkana Phantom Killer." YouTube. https://youtu.be/87y1_IbJRZE.

"Hot Wood Fire." Reference.com. https://www.reference.com/science/hot-wood-fire-902305ee9dfd05a4.

"The Hook." Snopes. https://www.snopes.com/fact-check/the-hook/?collection-id=209633.

"Lovers Lane." Hunt A Killer. https://members.huntakiller.com/blog-articles/lovers-lane.

"The Phantom Killer." Texas Ranger. https://texasranger.pastperfectonline.com/webobject/E0C9D686-43A8-4AFB-856C-900091633336.

Presley, James. The Phantom Killer.

Stockton, Christine. "13 Creepy Facts About The Texarkana Phantom Killer." Thought Catalog, 2020. https://thoughtcatalog.com/christine-stockton/2020/12/13-creepy-facts-about-the-texarkana-phantom-killer/.

"The Texarkana Phantom Moonlight Murders." Unsolved Casebook. https://www.unsolvedcasebook.com/the-texarkana-phantom-moonlight-murders/.

Haunted Spring, Texas

Season 1, Episode 8

Title: Bugs

Dropped: January 14, 2021

In Bugs, often touted as one of the worst episodes of Supernatural, Bugs used the trope of a Native American Curse. The said-to-be-haunted town of Spring, Texas, also has the idea of "cursed lands" attached to its lore.

The town of Spring, Texas, is located approximately 20 miles north of Houston along I-45 and is said to be one of the most haunted towns in Texas. The first known settlers of the Spring area were the Orcoquiza, also known as the Akokisa, Accokesaws, or Arkokisa, who established a winter camp there. They are believed to have inhabited five villages along the lower reaches of the Trinity and San Jacinto rivers, as well as the northern and eastern shores of Galveston Bay. In the early 18th century, explorers noted around 3,500 Orcoquiza living in the Houston area. However, by the mid-19th century, most had either merged with other tribes or succumbed to the ravages of Western diseases.

Colonists began to settle the area in the 1820s and established a trading post in 1838. In 1871, when the railroad came through, the workers named the site "Camp Spring" after enduring a brutal winter. Over time, the "camp" was dropped, and the town came to be known simply as Spring. By 1910, Spring had developed significantly, boasting a sugar mill, two cotton gins, five saloons, an opera house, a hospital, a bank, hotels, three churches, schools, and even a gambling hall. However, the town faced a downturn in the early 20th century, suffering from the aftermath of the devastating 1915 Galveston hurricane, followed by the Great Depression. Fortunately, prosperity returned with the Texas Oil Boom of the 1960s. With such a long history, it's said that some residents and visitors of Spring never truly leave. Legend has it that nearly every building in town is haunted, though many were relocated to Old

Spring from other towns. Some notable highlights include:

Spring State Bank

The Spring State Bank is said to be one of the most haunted buildings in town. Spring built its first bank in 1910, but that burned down in 1917. Legend has it that the Orcoquiza cursed the land when they were pushed out, proclaiming, "If anyone cuts down a tree or builds anything here, there will be a fire." This 1917 fire was just one of many. Guides on Ghost Tours in town will tell you that any shop owner in Old Town Spring who tries to make improvements or build additions experiences fires. The bank was rebuilt in another location, and that bank is said to have been robbed by the infamous Clyde Barrow. It became a laundromat in the 1970s, but it also caught fire. At the time of the episode recording, Mallot's Hardware and Variety Store stood there.

Signs of haunting include mysterious noises throughout the building. Paranormal teams have captured photos of mist and maybe full apparitions. A psychic reported that a big-nosed man is haunting the place, who once tried to stop the robberies.

Hudson's Whitehall

Hudson's Whitehall house is one of the original homes built in 1895 by the Mintz family. In those 100-plus years, it's seen some residents. A sign outside reads:

> Built in 1895
> 1900s Mrs. McGowan's Boarding House
> 1920s Klein Resident
> 1930s Funeral Home
> 1940s Converted into apartments, WWII
> 1950s Church and School House
> 1960s Hippie Commune
> 1970s Commercial Offices

During its time as a funeral home, in 1933, a young man drove off a bridge and hit a ravine. He and his date did not survive and were taken to Whitehall. This couple has become known as the "courting ghosts of Whitehall".

Paranormal activity observed at this house includes: general noise, moving objects, and full-body apparitions of the courting ghosts swinging on the upstairs porch.

During renovations, violent paranormal activity in a second-story room led to a lease clause: the room must remain undisturbed, and hauntings are not grounds for breaking the lease.

Train Tracks

The train tracks are largely responsible for there even being a town, but they are also the site of many of its tragedies, including:

> 1915: Hurricane destroyed the train depot
>
> 1921: A steam engine neared the crossing derailed
>
> 1974: A gasoline truck got hit by an oncoming train (2 fatalities)
>
> 2007: A van was hit by the train, causing 3 fatalities
>
> 2015: 13 cars derailed not far from the crossing (no fatalities)

People have reported seeing weird lights on the tracks, as well as orbs and shadow figures. The signal lights will come on even when no train is coming. One guy thought he saw an oncoming train so he stopped. There was no sound. But then he felt a rush of cold air and a headless man in overalls approached, waving a lantern (which is weird, because there is a similar sighting on the Ghost road in Saratoga, which isn't THAT far from there, about an hour away).

Wunsche Brothers

Carl Wunsche Sr., from one of Spring's German immigrant families, first bought the property in 1862. A cafe had previously existed on the land, but a tornado destroyed it. The Wunches Brothers, Dell and Willie, opened their saloon in 1902, the building constructed from their former mill and wood salvaged from the cafe mentioned above. Dell and Willie are said to be still hanging around the barn.

Once a hotel, a brothel, and a saloon, this building had its moments. It was notably the last bar shut down by Harris County when Prohibition began, the liquor violently destroyed by the Texas Rangers.

Legend has it that the spirit of Charlie Wunsche, also known as Uncle Charlie, a man who died with unrequited love, is particularly associated with the location. An artist who stayed in Uncle Charlie's room experienced a disturbing dream of a distressed man pacing back and forth. His sketch of this figure turned out to be a striking resemblance to Uncle Charlie himself.

Staff members have reported eerie encounters, including being touched and witnessing full-body apparitions. Disturbances have included telephone receivers being thrown off the wall, unexpected changes in music, and water turning on and off sporadically. Rearranging furniture often leads to mysterious occurrences, such as items being moved, doors locking on their own, and tables and chairs toppling.

At the time this episode aired, the building was undergoing reconstruction after a fire, but it has since reopened to the public.

Select Sources

Nance, Cathy. Haunted Old Town Spring. Haunted America, 2017.

"Old Town Spring Doll hospital." YouTube, https://youtu.be/1dXeFWps7LQ.

"Old Town Spring: Ghost in the Bank." Hollow Hill, https://hollowhill.com/old-town-spring-ghost-in-the-bank/.

"The Curse of Old Town Spring." South Writ Large, https://southwritlarge.com/articles/the-curse-of-old-town-spring/.

"The Spring Creek Context: Early History of Spring, Texas." Houston History Magazine, July 2013, https://houstonhistorymagazine.org/wp-content/uploads/2013/07/spring-creek.pdf.

"Wunsche Brothers Café: Haunted hotel in Old Town Spring?" YouTube, accessed October 20, 2025, https://www.youtube.com/watch?v=X5Hjl700M-c.

Poltergeist/Gef the Talking Mongoose

Season 1, Episode 9

Title: Home

Dropped: January 21, 2021

Thanks to the effervescent psychic, Missouri, we learn that the house in this episode isn't just haunted; it has attracted a poltergeist. And I just love the story of Gef, the Talking Mongoose.

Poltergeists are thought to be unconscious telekinetic activity linked to a person going through some emotional issue (e.g., teenagers) or a change in location or illness. Activity usually lasts a short period (one day to six years) and can move from one location to another. The activity is divided into stages:
1. Poltergeist-lite activity. The activity is easy to dismiss or explain away, such as night noises like scratching or cold

spots. This stage may be missed or skipped.

2. Activity demands more attention. Sounds are louder and out of the ordinary (e.g, knocking).

3. Can occur concurrently with Stage 2. During this phase, objects levitate, move, disappear, and reappear. There can be electrical malfunctions or the sudden appearance of water or fluids. Messages or pictures can appear on the walls or in mirrors. Stones may be thrown with varying frequency and violence, but most poltergeists seem to prefer a random approach. Poltergeist stone throwing is called *lithobolia*.

4. During this phase, objects "apport" (appear from nowhere) and "disapport" (vanish into nothingness).

5. Physical activity from the entity onto a person. People have reported being touched, pushed, slapped, and bitten.

6. Communication between a poltergeist entity and a human can occur. This can come as a disembodied voice or be directed (e.g., rapping once for yes, twice for know," the alphabet, etc.).

7. The Climax of the activity. This will likely be very noticeable and the most extreme display of activity. The entity may announce that it is going to leave if communication is occurring.

8. The activity will eventually come to an end. This often occurs when the circumstances surrounding the main person change (e.g, puberty hormones mellow out).

Gef, the Talking Mongoose aka The Dalby Spook

In the 1930s, on the Isle of Man, in the town of Dalby, there was a house where James ("Jim") and Margaret Irving lived with their 13-year-old daughter, Voirrey. They began hearing noises which made them think an animal was in the wall - scratching, barking, etc. Jim decided to growl at whatever was making the noise, and it growled back. This led to sounds on demand. Sounds became words - from baby talk to conversations. It squeakily repeated the nursery rhymes Voirrey told it. One day, the wall creature told them he was in fact a mongoose named "Gef" from New Delhi, and not just any mongoose, "an extra extra special mongoose." The Irvings were informed that Gef could speak this whole time, and "If you knew what I know, you'd know a hell of a lot!" Jim and Margaret were allowed to see Gef and described him as having a "long bushy tail and a yellowish hue with brown tail speckles and thought at first to resemble a weasel."

Gef began to sleep (do ghost mongooses sleep?) in a box in Voirrey's room. Gef was said to enjoy singing songs and taking the bus back and forth into town. Gef would indicate the conversation was over by shouting "vanished!" and then disappearing. He could be helpful, even doing basic chores, but warned, "If you are kind to me, I will bring you good luck. If you are not kind, I shall kill all your poultry. I can get them wherever you put them!" He seemed to have a warped sense of humor, calling Jim "fat-headed gnome" and shocking Margaret's sensibilities with dirty songs.

Gef started making claims of deityhood, such as "The Holy Ghost" and "The 8th Wonder of the World," and claimed to be from "the 5th

Dimension." He would say he was an earthbound spirit, but when asked if he was a spirit, he would reply: "If I were a spirit, I could not kill rabbits."

The activity escalated, and the language became more profane. Gef was said to belt out off-key tunes all night. Once, he sang for nearly an hour in the middle of the night, after which he exclaimed, "I did it for devilment!" Things became even less fun as the family could hear shrill screams and violent pounding on the wall, which seemed to move around the room.

Gef became a minor celebrity, and reporters came to the Isle to try to capture proof of the creature; the moniker "The Dalby Spook" was coined. The renowned psychic investigator Harry Price, along with Rex Lambert, founding editor of The BBC's *Listener* magazine, came to conduct an investigation. Analysis of hair samples, said to be from Gef, indicated they were from a "longish-haired dog." Price sent clay paw prints, believed to be from Gef, to Reginald Peacock at the Natural History Museum, who concluded they were not made by a mongoose, but possibly by a dog.

The Irving family moved away, and a new owner bought their farm. It appears that Gef did not follow the Irvings to their new home on the mainland, but his appearances had slowly become fewer and farther between even before they left. Gef also did not make himself known to the new owner of the home, but in 1947, a Mr. Graham claimed to have shot. He killed a strange animal on the property that was described as looking like neither a stoat, ferret, nor mongoose, and about which the farmer said, "It answers to all descriptions." When Graham moved away, the house was demolished.

Select Sources

Hamiltonparanormal.com. "Poltergeist."
Hamilton Paranormal, https://
hamiltonparanormal.com/poltergeist.html.

Josiffe, Christopher. Gef!: The Strange Tale of
an Extra-Special Talking Mongoose. Publish
Date: June 30th, 2017.

Matthews, Rupert. Poltergeists: And Other
Hauntings. United Kingdom, Arcturus
Publishing, 2018.

Mysteriousuniverse.org. "The Bizarre Saga of
Gef the Talking Mongoose." Mysterious
Universe, 11 August 2016, https://
mysteriousuniverse.org/2016/08/the-bizarre-
saga-of-gef-the-talking-mongoose/.

Spookyisles.com. "Poltergeist Haunting
Stages." Spooky Isles, https://
www.spookyisles.com/poltergeist-haunting-
stages/.

The Mental Floss. "The Strange Story of Gef
the Talking Mongoose." Mental Floss, 26
October 2015, https://www.mentalfloss.com/

Danvers State Hospital

Season 1, Episode 10

Title: Asylum

Dropped January 27, 2021

If you search the Internet for "haunted asylum," Danvers will no doubt appear in your results. Given its past, it's not shocking that it remains spooky AF.

In 1878, construction began on the Danvers Lunatic Asylum, later known as the Danvers State Hospital, in Massachusetts. Danvers was once known as Salem Village, and this was the actual site of the Salem Witch Trials. The hospital, nicknamed "the Witches' Castle," was built on Hathorne Hill, the former home of Judge John Hathorne, who presided over the trials. Initially projected to cost $600,000, the final cost soared to $1.5 million by the time of completion. Its gothic architecture is said to have inspired H.P. Lovecraft's Arkham Sanatorium, which, in turn, influenced the creation of Arkham

Asylum in DC's Batman comics. Initially, there were four buildings, separated by gender, divided by the administration building. It was built for 500 patients, but as numbers swelled to 2000, more buildings were added, and patients were even housed in the basement. At its peak, the property had 40 buildings.

The Kirkbride Plan
In its early days, Danvers State Hospital emerged as one of the most advanced institutions of its kind in the country, dedicated to providing comprehensive treatment for mental illness. Its first administrator, Thomas Kirkbride, aimed to create a humane and compassionate environment for patients, believing that beautiful surroundings could help restore a natural "balance of the senses." This vision became known as the Kirkbride Plan, which emphasized that most individuals with mental illness are curable, positioning the hospital's role primarily as a curative facility rather than merely custodial. The healing process was to be significantly enhanced by pleasant surroundings, fresh air, and clean water.

Patients engaged in farming and greenhouse activities while also maintaining the facilities, including the construction of small buildings on the property. They crafted shoes, did various crafts, and participated in Montessori kindergarten exercises. In the 1900s, they enjoyed weekly dances and were entertained with readings and music. By the 1930s, the hospital established a personal hygiene department offering haircuts, shampoos, manicures, and massages, along with a full-time on-site dentist.

Good intentions aside, the hospital was unable to keep pace with demand. As early as the 1900s, wards housed between 50 and 60 patients, far exceeding the recommended maximum of 35, particularly in the more chaotic wards. As patient numbers swelled, cots were placed in hallways and day rooms, forcing some patients to sleep in these areas. By the late 1930s, the hospital reached full capacity, accommodating over 2,600 patients. The staff struggled to manage the influx of unruly individuals who, at times, became violent. Some patients were left to roam the halls in a state of undress, often covered in their own waste.

Treatment

Some say Danvers State Hospital was the birthplace of the prefrontal lobotomy; they are wrong. However, Walter Freeman, the neurosurgeon who developed the standard prefrontal lobotomy technique, did perform over 200 lobotomies there. His procedure involved the not-so-surgically precise technique of poking a rod into the corner of the eye, wiggling it a bit, and then removing it. The results would be a calm patient — or, more accurately, a calm zombie.

The Hydrotherapy Department was established in 1936, based on the belief that water could alleviate the "clogged conditions" of the brain. This encompassed the use of water in all its forms—ice, liquid, or vapor—applied both internally and externally. Throughout the 1940s and 50s, patients at Danvers were subjected to shock therapy, psychosurgery, and a significant increase in lobotomies, paving the way for these procedures to spread to other hospitals nationwide.

By the 1950s, the introduction of new medications began to transform the treatment of mental illness, leading to a gradual decrease in overcrowding; however, visitors to the hospital at that time observed patients wandering in the halls or staring vacantly at the walls.

Hauntings

Jeralyn Levasseur, the child of an administrator in the 1940s and 50s, often encountered an apparition of an angry older woman during her childhood. Her nights were frequently disturbed by the spirit tugging at the covers of her bed. Others have reported hearing disembodied voices, wails, and patients calling for help and attention. Apparitions have been seen by those who stayed in nearby apartments, who described encounters with nightgown-clad figures standing against the walls of dark hallways, seemingly lost in thought. However, if approached, these figures vanish.

Among the most chilling Electronic Voice Phenomena (EVPs) recorded are a spirit declaring, "I live here," and another ominously stating, "I am warning you." Witnesses have also reported hearing unsettling whispers pleading for assistance, begging to "keep her away." This "her" has been described on multiple occasions as a slender, scowling woman dressed in Victorian-era clothing. Randomly appearing, she often stands menacingly in dimly lit corridors and charges at those she encounters.

Ghost hunters and former hospital staff have reported sightings of Thomas Kirkbride's ghost wandering through the underground tunnels, and I am not really surprised that tunnels running underneath a former mental institution are creepy. Numerous illnesses among ghost hunters and other enthusiasts who illegally toured the facility have raised concerns about an unknown toxin, as cited during the 2006 legal proceedings regarding the site's demolition. Residents of the nearby apartments now claim to hear moans and screams at night. Police officers responding to complaints about these unsettling noises often find only a desolate, empty lot, yet the eerie sounds are said to persist night after night.

Select Sources

"1.10 Asylum." Supernatural Wiki, http://www.supernaturalwiki.com/1.10_Asylum.

"A Brief History of Riverview Hospital." CBC News, 18 Dec. 2014, https://www.cbc.ca/news/canada/british-columbia/riverview-hospital-a-brief-history-1.2876488.

"Asylum Projects: Danvers State Hospital." Asylum Projects, http://www.asylumprojects.org/index.php?title=Danvers_State_Hospital.

"Cash Settlement for Sterilized Women." CBC News, 18 July 2011, https://www.cbc.ca/news/canada/british-columbia/cash-settlement-for-sterilized-women-1.565802.

"Creepy Ghost Places: Danvers State Hospital." Anomalien, https://anomalien.com/creepy-ghost-places-danvers-state-hospital/.

"Danvers State Hospital." FrightFind, https://frightfind.com/danvers-state-hospital/.

"Danvers State Hospital." Haunted Rooms, https://www.hauntedrooms.com/massachusetts/haunted-places/danvers-state-hospital.

"Danvers State Hospital." HorrorFacts, https://horrorfacts.com/danvers-state-hospital/.

"Danvers State Hospital History." Danvers State Hospital, https://www.danversstatehospital.org/history.

"Danvers State Hospital." Haunted Hovel, http://www.hauntedhovel.com/danversstatehospital.html.
"Danvers State Mental Hospital Inside & Out." YouTube, https://youtu.be/4qV9AOh8UFs.

"How Long Does It Take for a Body to Decompose?" Crime Scene Cleanup, https://www.crimescenecleanup.com/how-long-does-it-take-for-a-body-to-decompose/.

"How Long Does It Take a Body to Decompose." Ranker, https://www.ranker.com/list/how-long-does-it-take-a-body-to-decompose/erin-wisti.

"Insane Asylums: America's Most Notorious Hauntings." Exemplore, https://exemplore.com/paranormal/Insane-Asylums-Americas-Most-Notorious-Hauntings.

"Riverview Hospital (Coquitlam, B.C.)." Coquitlam Archives, http://searcharchives.coquitlam.ca/index.php/informationobject/browse?page=3&collection=1809&topLod=0&view=card&onlyMedia=1&sort=alphabetic.

"Smell of Death: Body Decomposition Odor & Cleanup." Aftermath, https://www.aftermath.com/content/body-decomposition-smell/.

"Smurl Haunting." Wikipedia, https://en.wikipedia.org/wiki/Smurl_haunting.

"This Creepy Abandoned Asylum In Massachusetts Is Straight Out Of A Horror Movie." Only In Your State, https://www.onlyinyourstate.com/massachusetts/insane-asylum-ma/.

"This Creepy Abandoned Asylum In Boston Is Straight Out Of A Horror Movie." Only In Your State, https://www.onlyinyourstate.com/massachusetts/boston/creepy-asylum-boston/.

Vanir

Season 1, Episode 11

Title: Scarecrow

Dropped: February 4, 2021

This episode had generic versions of the Vanir gods, and barely touched on much of the actual Norse mythology. I wish they had touched more on the magic side of things, but that's just me.

The Vanir are one of the two primary groups of gods in Norse mythology (the other being the Æsir). Historical accounts of their worship are sparse, possibly because certain practices were deemed offensive by the uptight folks documenting history.

Pantheon Highlights

The god Njord (Njordor)

Njord is the god of wind and sea, and is associated with rain, sunshine, harvests, and overall abundance. Both sailors and hunters invoked his aid. Njord fathered Freyr and Freyja with his sister.

Freyr

Freyr is the principal male god of fertility, particularly connected to the horse cult. Neigh. His phallic symbolism underscores his status as a fertility deity.

When Freyr travels, he is accompanied by his trusted boar, Gullinbursti, and a ship named Skidbladnir, which he can fold small enough to fit into a pouch. Freyr's sacred animals include both the horse and the boar, the latter of which he shares with his sister, Freyja, who is also known as Syr, meaning sow. My brother was mercilessly called a pig's name by his cousins as a child, too, Freyja. The boar is sometimes called Gold-Bristles, and the Horse "Bloody Hoof."

Freya

Freya remains a fairly well-known goddess. At the time of this recording, Freya was among the most popular baby girl names. Fun fact:

sometimes she's not just Freyr's sister; she is also his wife.

In one of the Eddic poems, Loki accuses Freya of having had romantic encounters with all the gods and elves, including her brother. While this could have been true, as a goddess of fertility, if she did sleep with everyone, that was just her nature, and the slut shaming is highly unnecessary.

While Freya embodies fertility and wealth, she is also a goddess of war. She is closely associated with cats; when she travels, she rides in a chariot pulled by cats.

Freya also has sacrificial associations; during the peace settlement between the Æsir and Vanir, Odin appointed her to oversee blood sacrifices. While sounding bloody, in this role, Freya helped create peace among the gods and maintained the world's essential cycles of fertility.

She has connections to magic and divination. In the Snorri translation of the Saga of Ynglings, Freyja brought seidr magic to the Æsir.

Seidr Magic and the Völva

The Vanir are the masters of seidr (*seiðr*) magic, and Freya taught the Æsir, including Odin, how to use it.

Seidr focuses on both divining and influencing fate and was practiced primarily in this realm during the Iron Age in Scandinavia. The primary practitioners were female seeresses, known as Völva. The male counterparts were known as Vitki. Burials for the Völva have been found throughout Scandinavia, indicating that they held significant positions in society.

A typical ritual involved a Völva entering a trance while other women chanted or drummed to summon her guardian spirit for assistance. While in the trance state, the spirits delivered to the Völva what amounted to a weather and news report. They offered insights into future occurrences, weather trends, and the destinies of both humans and animals. The practitioner could also astral project to other realms to seek knowledge while in this state.

The colorfully dressed Völva traveled through the countryside, sharing their predictions with the locals along the way. In the "Saga of Eric the Red," the Völva is described as wearing the skins of various creatures. She is depicted wearing a hood and gloves lined with cat skin and consuming the hearts of all available living beings. They were also well known for their staffs or wands, used for Seidr magic. Eventually, the Church banned staffs and wands. Those found with them were punished by death for practicing magic.

Select Sources

"1.11 Scarecrow." Supernatural Wiki,
www.supernaturalwiki.com/1.11_Scarecrow.

"Among Trees, Bones, and Stones: The
Sacred Grove at Lunda."
https://www.academia.edu/14914702/
Among_trees_bones_and_stones_the_sacred
_grove_at_Lunda.

Crawford, Jackson. "Wagon of the Vanir God."
YouTube video, 10:23. September 22, 2017.
https://youtu.be/crOzii_iiNo.

Crawford, Jackson W. https://
jacksonwcrawford.com/.

"Dísablót: A Norse Fall Festival", YouTube,
https://youtu.be/OGWZGvpk-aw.

"Freyja, Goddess of Abundance, Fertility, and
War." Learn Religions. https://
www.learnreligions.com/freyja-goddess-of-
abundance-fertility-war-2561963.

"Freya." Mythopedia. https://mythopedia.com/
norse-mythology/gods/freya/.

"Freyr." Skjalden. https://skjalden.com/freyr/.

Grimfrost. https://grimfrost.com/.

Hall, Erich S. "Blót." Asatru. http://www.erichshall.com/asanew/blot.htm.

"Historical Worship of the Norse Gods", YouTube, https://youtu.be/qv8UVW3mBhw.

"Njord." Mythopedia. https://mythopedia.com/norse-mythology/gods/njord/.

"Norse Gods Names", YouTube, https://youtu.be/4GcUphVrMjE.

"Rällinge statuette." Wikipedia. https://en.wikipedia.org/wiki/R%C3%A4llinge_statuette#CITEREFAnderssonBeronius_J%C3%B6rpelandDun%C3%A9r 2003.

"Seiðr", Norse Mythology, https://norse-mythology.org/concepts/seidr/.

"Stone Phalluses and Ancient Fertility Cults." Norwegian SciTech News, 13 Feb. 2015, norwegianscitechnews.com/2015/02/stone-phalluses-and-ancient-fertility-cults/.

"The Ancient Cult of the Wagon Goddess." English History Authors. September 24, 2015. https://englishhistoryauthors.blogspot.com/2015/09/the-ancient-cult-of-wagon-goddess.html.

"The Story of Saint Olaf and the Viking Horse." Little Red Umbrella, 15 Dec. 2010, www.littleredumbrella.com/2010/12/story-of-saint-olaf-and-viking-horse.html

"The Vǫlva (Norse Seeress) and Seiðr", YouTube, https://youtu.be/pPPWde7SVk0.

"Vanir Cult." Earth and Starry Heaven. December 19, 2018. https://earthandstarryheaven.com/2018/12/19/vanir-cult/.

"Vanir." Mythology Wiki. https://mythology.wikia.org/wiki/Vanir.

"Völva: The Viking Witch or Seeress." Skjalden, skjalden.com/volva-the-viking-witch-or-seeress/.

Rawhead and Bloody Bones/ Tarot

Season 1, Episode 12

Title: Faith

Dropped: February 11, 2021

Sam and Dean hunt a rawhead, a leather-skinned boogeyman preying on children. Also, Sam pulls out a tarot deck with the cross he saw on the altar. Sams says, "Tarot dates back to the early Christian era, when some priests were still using magic? And a few of them veered into the dark stuff? Necromancy and how to push death away, how to cause it?" That didn't sound quite right so I had to look it up.

Bloody Bones and his companion Rawhead are figures from British folklore, appearing in England as early as the 16th century. Rawhead could have developed as a metaphor for smallpox, still common in the 16th century. Smallpox frequently led to pustules covering the entire head; it's understandable how someone with advanced smallpox would develop a "raw head." When the story migrated to North America, it became ingrained in the South, where it transformed into Rawhead and Bloody Bones.

Given its longevity, it's not surprising that there are several versions of this lore. In some, Rawhead is a water creature, lurking below the surface in murky ponds and flooded gravel pits, dragging the unwary down into the depths to feast on, a story likely created as a warning to keep children from drowning. In other land-based versions, Rawhead lives in cupboards and under stairs. If you peek between your ankles into the space between stairs, especially stairs leading down into a basement, you might see Rawhead sitting on a pile of bones, waiting to reach out and grab your ankles as happened to Sam in this episode.

In the most popular American versions, Rawhead is depicted as a razorback boar with a gross snout and distinctive red markings, who is also the sole companion of Old Betty, a "conjure woman" living the dream swamp-witch life alone in the swamp or deep woods. After a man eats Rawhead to spite her, Old Betty conjures Rawhead's spirit from the other side, creating *Rawhead and Bloody Bones*, a creature with a humanoid body and a boar's skull for a head, dripping in blood. Rawhead and Bloody Bones stalk their killer, often engaging in a question-and-answer game, as in Little Red Riding Hood. For example, the hunter asks the creature about its "foul red eyes," and it responds, "the better to see your grave," and then eats him. After this, Rawhead and Bloody Bones decides he likes eating things, especially children, and haunts the woods looking for naughty kids for his next meal. It is unclear what happened to Old Betty, but I assume she continued living her best life.

Tarot and Necromancy
When does Tarot date back to?
While the exact origins and date of the Tarot's introduction are debated, Italian playing cards from the 14th and 15th centuries form the basis of what would become the modern Tarot deck. These cards evolved to include

additional "triumph" cards, expanding on the original four-suit deck of batons, coins, cups, and swords, and were used for trick-taking games. The earliest surviving complete tarot deck, the *Sola Busca* tarot, dates back to the 15th century. It does not have the standard Major Arcana, but instead features historical figures, such as the Roman Emperor Nero.

Tarot has waxed and waned in popularity as an occult tool. *Le Monde Primitif*, written by Court de Gebeline in 1781, proposed that Tarot cards originated in the Egyptian *Book of Thoth* and were spread throughout Europe by the Romani or other travelers. In 1791, Etteilla (Jean-Baptiste Alliette), a French occultist, published what is considered the first Tarot deck and book set.

The Rider Waite Deck, first released in 1910, is probably the most recognized tarot deck today. Each card features illustrations of the divinatory meaning by Golden Dawn member Pamela Coleman Smith, and this is the first known version to specify the meaning of the Minor Arcana.

Select Sources

"Bloody Bones." Monster Wiki, Fandom, https://monster.fandom.com/wiki/Bloody_Bones.

"Bloody Bones: A History of Southern Scares." Deep South Magazine, 17 Oct. 2014, https://deepsouthmag.com/2014/10/17/bloody-bones-a-history-of-southern-scares/.

"Folklore's Scariest Creatures: Rawhead and Bloody Bones." Writing Werewolf, 11 June 2020, https://writingwerewolf.wordpress.com/2020/06/11/folklores-scariest-creatures-rawhead-and-bloody-bones/.

"Raw-Head & Bloody Bones." GrannySue, 25 Nov. 2008, https://grannysu.blogspot.com/2008/11/raw-head-bloody-bones.html.

"Raw-Head, Bloody-Bones and other terrors of the nursery." Oxford English Dictionary, public.oed.com/blog/raw-head-bloody-bones-and-other-terrors-of-the-nursery/.

"Rawhead and Bloody Bones." Mask of Reason, https://maskofreason.wordpress.com/the-book-of-mysteries/know-your-ghosts/europe/rawhead-and-bloody-bones/.

"Rawhead and Bloody Bones." Reckless Tea, 26 Jan. 2019, https://recklesstea.wordpress.com/2019/01/26/rawhead-and-bloody-bones/.

"Sweat." Xroads, University of Virginia, xroads.virginia.edu/~MA01/Grand-Jean/Hurston/Chapter10.html.

"Why Did Rawhead Scare Kids So?" Appalachian History, 16 Oct. 2020, https://www.appalachianhistory.net/2020/10/why-did-rawhead-scare-kids-so.html.

"A History of Tarot Cards, from the Italian Renaissance to Fortune-Telling." National Geographic. https://www.nationalgeographic.com/history/article/tarot-cards-history-fortune-telling.

"The Colorful History of Tarot: Mesmerizing as the Decks Themselves." Smithsonian Magazine. https://www.smithsonianmag.com/arts-culture/colorful-history-tarot-mesmerizing-decks-themseles-180986811/.

"The Crazy History of Necromancy Explained." Grunge. https://www.grunge.com/251326/the-crazy-history-of-necromancy-explained.

"Etteilla." Wikipedia. https://en.wikipedia.org/wiki/Etteilla.

"Etteilla, the first modern card reader and his reconstructed decks by Marco Benedetti." Tarot Heritage. April 9, 2024. https://tarot-heritage.com/2024/04/09/etteilla-the-first-modern-card-reader-and-his-reconstructed-decks-by-marco-benedetti/.

"History of Tarot Cards." HowStuffWorks. https://entertainment.howstuffworks.com/horoscopes-astrology/history-of-tarot-cards.htm.

"RAWHEAD AND BLOODY BONES."
Sciencia. https://www.sciencia.cat/temes/
medieval-necromancy-art-controlling-demons.

"Tarot." Wikipedia. https://en.wikipedia.org/
wiki/Tarot.

Haunted Clinton Road

Season 1, Episode 13

Title: Route 666

Dropped February 18, 2021

I went searching for haunted roads, and Clinton Road is what I found. So have all the YouTubers.

Named after the now-vanished settlement of Clinton, Clinton Road has been called the most haunted road in America. It stretches for 10 miles in West Milford, Passaic County, New Jersey, beginning at NJ Route 23. According to Weird New Jersey's J. Percy Crayon, the legends date back to at least 1905, "It was never advisable to pass through the 'five mile woods' after dark, for tradition tells us they were infested with bands of robbers and counterfeiters, not to mention the witches who held their nightly dances and carousels at Green Island, along with the ghosts that appeared in frightful forms, more terrifying to the peaceful inhabitants than wild animals or even the Indians who often passed through." You had me at witches dancing in the woods. Here are some of the urban legends associated with Clinton Road:

Cross Castle

Deep in the woods off Clinton Road, a three-story castle-like structure was built in 1905 by Richard Cross for his wife and children. After Cross died in 1917, the family sold the property to the City of Newark. Over time, a fire ravaged much of the wooden structure, leaving only the stone walls standing. During its decline, the site became a gathering place for Satanists and the KKK, allegedly. The walls, once adorned with graffiti, although stripped for souvenirs, were torn down in 1988 after the Newark Watershed Commission deemed the structure unsafe.

Also, according to local legend, the castle mysteriously rebuilds itself every October 30th, with the KKK rumored to perform goat sacrifices on that night.

Clinton Ironworks

Many people mistakenly believe it to be a Druid creation or a temple associated with the occult. Constructed in the early 1800s, this pyramid-shaped structure was once part of a brief iron-making community, likely created because after the wars with the British, America needed to make money and its own iron. An early 19th-century village was created to support an iron industrial complex, that ceased operations in 1852. Today, the structure is enclosed by a chain-link fence but is easily visible from the road.

Dead Man's Curve and Ghost Boy

Dead Man's Curve is the sharpest curve on Clinton Road. This stretch of road has been linked to nearly every type of paranormal activity, including ghosts and UFOs.

There is also a bridge over Clinton Brook, where a ghost boy will either throw back coins you toss over into the water or push you into the water if you put a quarter into the middle of the road.

Ghost Truck!?

There is supposed to be a black truck hiding in the shadows of Clinton Road. There are some videos of this happening on the Internet. The truck appears seemingly out of thin air, tailgates you, flashes its lights, then disappears. I do not know if this is a ghost or a jerk, but this is a dick move. Don't be a dick, ghost truck.

Cryptids?

Several strange animals have been sighted on Clinton Road—everything from hellhounds to monkeys. Rumor has it an animal attraction shut down and let its animals loose.

Some Facts

According to New Jersey state transportation records, between 2007 and 2011, 51 accidents near the Route 23-Clinton Road intersection resulted in one fatality and 17 injuries, and 12 of the drivers involved were under the age of 20.

Select Sources

"Clinton Road." Wikipedia, Wikimedia Foundation, https://en.wikipedia.org/wiki/Clinton_Road_(New_Jersey.

"Creepy, Cursed, and Curvy: New Jersey's Clinton Road Is the Most Frightening Road in America." New York Daily News, 21 May 2014, https://www.nydailynews.com/autos/creepy-cursed-curvy-new-jersey-clinton-road-frightening-road-america-article-1.1803331.

Grossman, Scott. "Teenage Girl Killed in West Milford Collision, 6 Injured." Grossman Justice, https://www.grossmanjustice.com/teenage-girl-killed-in-west-milford-collision-6-injured.

"Paranormal History: Clinton Road, NJ." Monstrum Athenaeum, http://monstrumathenaeum.org/paranormal-history-clinton-road-nj/.

"REVISED: CLINTON ROAD." Roadtrippers, https://maps.roadtrippers.com/trips/15740010.

"Ringwood Manor Historic District." NPGallery, National Park Service, https://npgallery.nps.gov/NRHP/GetAsset/NRHP/76001179_text.

"Weird NJ: Clinton Road." Weird NJ, https://weirdnj.com/stories/clinton-road/.

Psychokinesis and the Military

Season 1, Episode 14

Title: Nightmare

Dropped: February 25, 2021

Would the government have conducted experiments on Max Miller? Maybe.

Psychokinesis (aka PK, aka telekinesis): the action of the mind on matter, in which objects are supposedly caused to move or change as a result of mental concentration upon them.
Throughout history, various military and government groups have researched psychic phenomena and psychokinesis, including the Nazis, Soviet Communists, and Americans, all of whom initiated their own programs. Most of the following is derived from Annie Jacobsen's book, Phenomena: The Secret History of the U.S. Government's Investigations Into Extrasensory Perception and Psychokinesis.
Various levels of the U.S. Government in the 1970s were operating on the premise that the Soviet Union was performing in-depth

research on psychic phenomena, including remote viewing and psychotronic torture. One reason for this was the Army's Sensitive Activity Vulnerability Estimates (SAVE) team, tasked with visiting various Army sites to identify exploitable vulnerabilities. This team included Second Lieutenant Fred Holmes Atwater, allegedly influenced by a report published for the Defense Intelligence Agency that hypothesized the Soviets might be using extrasensory perception (ESP) for espionage and psychokinesis to disrupt weapon systems. The content of this study emphasized the activities of Warsaw Pact countries in paranormal informational processes—such as telepathy, clairvoyance, and remote viewing— as well as paranormal energetic processes — such as psychokinesis and bioenergetics.

Atwater advocated that the Army establish a unit at Fort Meade to train intelligence professionals in counterintelligence operations, enabling them to become remote viewers, which led to the establishment of Project Gondola Wish in 1977, later rebranded as Grill Flame. The civilian partner for this initiative was SRI International. The unit consisted of six members, selected from over

2,000 candidates, including Warrant Officer Joe McMoneagle, three civilian Army employees, and two intelligence officers. This project had a notably unconventional vibe for the military; due to its clandestine nature, team members could dress in civilian clothing and wear long hair, and could embrace practices such as yoga and mural painting. Regardless, they were called on to provide "critical" information to the National Security Council, the CIA, and the Joint Chiefs of Staff during the Iran hostage crisis.

The Advanced Human Technology Office
Major General Albert Stubblebine, an advocate for psychic warfare, was appointed commanding general of the U.S. Army Intelligence and Security Command (INSCOM) in 1981. In what would one day become a superhero movie plot, Stubblebine initiated a project within INSCOM to develop a "super soldier" capable of becoming invisible at will and walking through walls. He even attempted to walk through walls himself with doubtful success. Stubblebine believed that everyone possesses ESP and PK traits and required all his battalion commanders to learn

spoon-bending, mimicking the semi-celebrity Uri Geller. He personally pursued several psychic feats, including levitation and the ability to disperse clouds with his mind. Stubblebine also established the Advanced Human Technology Office, led by Lt. Colonel John B. Alexander, a former Green Beret and special forces commander. Alexander, who held a PhD in education from Walden University (though he was interested in thanatology, the study of death), researched spiritual change among participants in a Kübler-Ross life, death, and transition workshop. Known as a leading advocate for non-lethal weapons and military applications of the paranormal, he has also written extensively on the reality of UFOs. Alexander authored the first article on extrasensory perception (ESP) and psychokinesis (PK) in an official U.S. Army publication titled "The New Mental Battlefield: Beam Me Up, Spock," which appeared in the magazine for the U.S. Army Combined Arms Center at Fort Leavenworth.

The Advanced Human Technology Office went around the country to learn what motivated people - they even went to the Dallas Cowboys. Then, because McMoneagle gained weight, the Army threatened to kick him out. Somehow, this led him to attend a new-age retreat at the Monroe Institute in the Blue Ridge Mountains. Soon, hundreds of INSCOM personnel followed McMoneagle, most eager to "expand their consciousness and have out-of-body experiences" through hemi-sync. This audio technique uses binaural beats to create unique auditory experiences.

In 1983, the Army Science Board held a retreat at the Monroe Institute to discuss strategies for enhancing human capability and performance; however, an external team assessed Monroe's methods and deemed them nonsense. The Defense Intelligence Agency consulted the CIA for its opinion, and the CIA, too, recommended against engaging with the Monroe Institute.

Simultaneously, in 1983, magician James Randi, who had a rivalry with the previously mentioned spoon-bender Uri Geller, placed two teenagers as moles at a privately funded McDonnell Laboratory for Psychical Research at Washington University. Over three years, they played pranks on the facility, ultimately revealing it as a "hoax." This revelation prompted the INSCOM Grill Fame to consult magicians, including the once-famous Doug Henning and Jack Houck, for their expertise.

In 1984, General Stubblebine took early retirement, and Brigadier General Harry Soyster, the new commander of INSCOM, canceled the remote viewing program. However, since the Secretary of the Army had authorized the program, only the Secretary of the Army had the power to terminate it officially. Thus, it remained in limbo until the DIA decided to absorb it and rebrand it as Sun Streak. Remote viewing continued until it evolved into STAR GATE in 1991. In 1995, the program transitioned from the DIA to the CIA, but following a report declaring that "remote viewing wasn't real," the CIA canceled and declassified the initiative. Over 20 years, more than $20 million was invested in this project.

The story may not be over. Annie Jacobsen noted that the Office of Naval Research currently (in 2017) has the Anomalous Mental Cognition initiative, a $3.9 million program established in 2014 to explore the possibility of precognition—often referred to colloquially as a "spidey sense." Under the banner of Perceptual Training Systems and Tools, what was once called extrasensory perception has been rebranded in modern times as "sense-making." According to official Defense Department literature, sense-making is defined as "a motivated, continuous effort to understand connections (which can be among people, places, and events) to anticipate their trajectories and act effectively."

Spoon Bending with Jack Houck

In 1981, Jack Houck, a systems engineer at Boeing Aerospace, and Severin Dahlen, a metallurgist from McDonnell Douglas Aerospace Company, began hosting spoon-bending parties in Manhattan Beach, CA. Their intriguing three-step protocol involved:

1. Establishing a mental connection with the object you wish to affect (the spoon).
2. Commanding the spoon to bend by enthusiastically shouting, "Bend! Bend! Bend!"

3. Letting go and allowing your mind to embrace the possibility of bending metal with your thoughts.

The results were impressive, with approximately 85 percent of the spoons bending successfully. Dahlen later analyzed the bent spoons in his lab and concluded that "stainless flatware appears to be the easiest metal to bend with psychokinesis." Over the course of more than 50 parties, around 1,000 participants bent various items, including hacksaw blades, silver-plated serving spoons, and five-sixteenth-inch steel rods.

Select Sources

"5 True Stories of the Military's Paranormal Activity Research." Task & Purpose, https:// taskandpurpose.com/history/5-true-stories-militarys-paranormal-activity-research/.

"Albert Stubblebine." Wikipedia, https:// en.wikipedia.org/wiki/Albert_Stubblebine.

"Beat (Acoustics) - Binaural Beats." Wikipedia, https://en.wikipedia.org/wiki/ Beat_(acoustics)#Binaural_beats.

Geller, Uri. "Not a Trick: Uri Geller, Mossad, CIA Agent." Uri Geller, https:// www.urigeller.com/not-trick-uri-geller-mossad-cia-agent/.

"Hemi-Sync." Wikipedia, https:// en.wikipedia.org/wiki/Hemi-Sync.

"How Project Star Gate Worked." Apple Podcasts, https://podcasts.apple.com/us/ podcast/how-project-star-gate-worked/ id278981407?i=1000477281006.

Houck, Jack. http://www.jackhouck.com/.

Jacobsen, Annie. "US Government Secret Investigations Into ESP (Extrasensory Perception)." CBS News, https://www.cbsnews.com/news/us-government-secret-investigations-into-esp-extrasensory-perception-annie-jacobsen/.

Jackobsen, Annie. Phenomena: The Secret History of the U.S. Government's Investigations into Extrasensory Perception and Psychokinesis. 2017.

"John B. Alexander." Wikipedia, https://en.wikipedia.org/wiki/John_B._Alexander.

"PARAPHYSICS RD - WARSAW PACT." The Black Vault, https://documents.theblackvault.com/documents/dia/PARAPHYSICS_RD-WARSAW_PACT.pdf.

"Paraphysics RD Warsaw Pact." Internet Archive, https://archive.org/details/ParaphysicsRDWarsawPact_201609.

"Phenomena." Time, https://time.com/
4721715/phenomena-annie-jacobsen/.

"Psychokinesis." Encyclopaedia Britannica,
https://www.britannica.com/topic/
psychokinesis.

"Stargate Project." Wikipedia, https://
en.wikipedia.org/wiki/Stargate_Project.

The Bloody Benders

Season 1, Episode 15

Title: The Benders

Dropped: March 4, 2021

I was surprised, as you were,, to learn that there really was a creepy serial-killer family called the Benders.

The story of the Benders, "America's first serial killer family," is one where it can be hard to distinguish fact from sensational journalism. At the time of their alleged crimes, numerous newspaper articles and other writings were produced. Still, they often contradict one another, and people were definitely trying to sell papers. What is known is that there was a family of four people called the Benders, who moved to Kansas in 1870 and 1871:

John, John Jr (Gebhert), Ma (sometimes given the first name Elvira), and Kate.

One Origin Story:

The Benders were driven out of a Pennsylvania German settlement because they were discovered to be witches: Mrs. Bender and Kate went out into a graveyard at midnight and got naked. They renounced Christianity, gave their bodies and souls to the devil. Then they banged a "dark stranger" and chanted things with him and said the Lord's Prayer backward and thus became witches.

More Likely Origin Story:

In 1870, two of the Benders arrived in Labette County, Kansas: John Bender, around 60 years old, and his younger counterpart, Johnny, approximately 25. Old John spoke English but with a heavy German accent. At the same time, Johnny communicated well in English, albeit with a noticeable accent and a tendency to giggle, which led some to label him a "half-wit."

The Benders purchased two tracts of land: 160 acres in the northeast corner of Osage Township and a smaller strip to the north, which featured a small pond for watering livestock. They constructed a modest 16x24-

foot house situated about 100 yards from the Osage Trail, complete with a cellar, a well, and a lean-to stable with a corral.

In 1871, Mrs. Bender arrived, speaking broken English and German but rarely engaging in conversation. Described as a heavyset woman with an unfriendly demeanor and sinister eyes, she quickly earned the nickname "she-devil" from her neighbors. Accompanying her was Kate, a young woman in her early twenties who spoke English fluently. Some stories say that John was not the father of the two younger Benders. And some even say that Johnny and Kate weren't brother and sister at all, but lovers.

The Benders converted the house into an inn or tavern, with a wagon canvas used to divide the space into two distinct areas: one for business and another for family life. Here, they sold various groceries to travelers, including tobacco, coffee, sardines, and ammunition. Guests could also enjoy a meal prepared by Ma and served by Kate, featuring dishes like cornbread and jackrabbit. Accommodation options included sleeping outside or on a simple pallet on the floor.

Mrs. Bender and Kate traveled throughout the area to heal the sick. Kate eventually turned this practice into a profession, creating cards and handbills to promote her services, some of which still exist today. Known as "Prof. Miss Katie Bender," she claimed to heal all sorts of diseases, including blindness, fits, deafness, and even deafness and dumbness. Her promotional materials included her address.

Kate was said to have a remarkable array of mystical talents. She could find lost articles, understand astrology and numerology, read palms, tell fortunes with sticks and buttons, cast spells on malicious women, and even sell lucky charms and love potions.

As the younger Benders became more social, they began attending church socials, private dances, Sunday School, and choir practice. The men were particularly fond of Kate, while the women were less enthusiastic. The local boys would often hang around the Bender place, helping with chores and buying groceries. They also assisted in selling horses, saddles, rigs, and other belongings left behind by travelers who couldn't pay in cash. A large number of travelers apparently were low on money during their travels.

Rumors and strange stories about the Benders started circulating through the area. One tale involved a woman who said she visited Kate multiple times in search of a cure for an illness. When the treatment took too long, she returned to demand a refund. Instead, Kate proposed a séance. During this, the family began speaking in incoherent gibberish while passing around a club, a knife, and a pistol. Terrified, the woman fled and did not share her experience until much later.

Another account described a woman interested in Spiritualism, a common practice at the time, who attended a séance at the Bender house. Kate and her brother drew human figures on the wall, then began stabbing them during the event. Kate proclaimed that the spirits commanded her to kill, prompting the woman to flee in justified fear.

This story is most likely a myth: Kate would visit a farmer two miles away, disguised as a cat. Once inside, she would transform into a woman, sleep with the farmer, and then change back into a cat to return home.

Bodies

In the fall of 1871, two boys discovered a body in a creek. Later, the remains were identified as William Jones, a stone mason traveling to Independence with a large sum of cash to buy land, who had never reached his destination.

The following year, a severe blizzard struck, and when the snow cleared, two more bodies emerged on the plains, clearly victims of a violent crime as their heads had been bludgeoned and their throats cut. They were never unidentified.

Throughout 1872, approximately eight more travelers went missing, all of whom were carrying money or valuable goods along the Osage Trail. Dr. York discovered George Loncher's absence after learning that the wagon and horses he had sold to him were found abandoned. Loncher was traveling with his 19-month-old daughter. When Dr. York went to investigate, he disappeared as well. His disappearance would prove to be a significant catalyst for investigating the crimes, as Dr. York's brother was a senator.

In April 1873, concerned locals hijacked the annual school board meeting to discuss the recent disappearances. The meeting had attracted around 75 to 100 people, including the male Benders, who decided to search all the camping sites in the area for the missing. If that yielded no results, they would begin searching the homesteads. Still, the locals took little action for several weeks.

Around the same time, Dr. York's brother, Colonel (Senator) York, organized a search party of 50 to 60 men to scour the area for his missing brother. The searchers learned that Dr. York's last known stop was buying cigars in Parsons. Based on this, they were informed he might have lodged at the Bender Inn for the night. When they visited the Benders, the family confirmed he had spent the night, but claimed he had left.

Kate Bender offered to enter a trance and consult her spirit guide, but requested a day or two for the process, asking the search party to return later. Dr. York's wife noted that Kate played the role of a spiritual medium, claiming to control the devil and warning that those who mocked her spiritual presentations would face dire consequences.

When the search party returned the next day, Kate lamented that her trance had failed. When the searchers inquired about a body found in the creek, young John Bender claimed he had also been ambushed at that very location but had managed to escape. As the searchers departed, some members wondered whether the Benders should be arrested, but Colonel York dismissed the idea, calling them simple folks who meant no harm.

On May 1, 1873, a neighbor of the Benders noticed several animals wandering around their property and realized that the Benders were missing. As word spread, a group gathered to search the property. One of the York brothers found his brother's glasses, while beneath the stove, they uncovered a handmade 6-pound sledgehammer, an Alsatian shoe hammer, and a 3-inch claw hammer. Strange designs and figures were scrawled on the floor, and under the dining room table, they discovered a door. When it was opened, a horrendous smell wafted out, leading the former soldiers to exclaim, "That is rotting blood!"

They pried the house off its foundation and discovered the floor and surrounding dirt soaked with blood, along with a passageway leading to the back of the house. After some time, they concluded that, while the scene was gross, there was no evidence and decided to leave. However, others began to notice what appeared to be graves in the orchard. They dug, and the first grave revealed who they believed to be Dr. York, whose head had been bashed and throat slashed. To confirm the identification, they severed the head from the corpse, cleaned it, and mounted it beside the grave. Edward York confirmed that it was his brother.

The following day, they unearthed eight more corpses, including George Loncher and his daughter. She bore no marks on her throat, and it is believed she suffocated, possibly while being buried beneath her father's body. Among the bodies were a man and a woman, never identified. In the weeks that followed, over a thousand people flocked to the house, taking pieces of it as souvenirs.

The town forcefully interrogated the Benders' German neighbor, Rudolph Brockman, who was infatuated with Kate Bender, even hanging him four times. Eventually, they gave up and left him alone. York's men were reported to have used hanging by the necks as a means to question those suspected of being involved or complicit, some pinpointed because they were deemed to be of ill repute or Spiritualists.

As time passed, accumulated stories led to a clearer understanding of the Benders' murder methodology and motives. The Benders likely stole what amounted to about $6,000 in 1870s cash, along with all the stolen goods sold by Kate's beaus in nearby towns. Most accounts suggest Kate was responsible, though it's debated whether she was truly the ringleader. As for methodology, it is believed that the

Benders lured travelers into the house, assessed their worth, and determined if they would live. Kate would charm the guests as they ate in front of the wagon canvas. While she distracted them, the victim would be struck from behind the canvas, probably with a sledgehammer. The victims were lowered through a trapdoor, and their throats slit. After dark, the Benders removed the bodies. Initially, they were left on the prairie, but when those remains were discovered too quickly, the Benders disposed of some bodies in a well, leading to the need for a second well. Eventually, they just buried the bodies in the orchard.

But where did they go? Nobody really knows. Governor and Colonel York offered a $3,000 reward for their whereabouts. One train station agent thought he remembered a German family traveling north. At the same time, another speculated they headed south, possibly making their way to Texas. They may even have split up. One of the prevailing tales suggests that a posse found them, killed them, and took their money.

Rumors about their fate persisted: Kate was spotted as a society matron in San Francisco, a sex worker in Montana, and an outlaw in several cities. One intriguing story comes from a Mexican captain named Don Pieppo, who claimed the family went to California, obtained a hot air balloon to travel to Mexico, but were swept out to sea by the winds, resulting in their demise—except for one survivor, John Bender Jr., who turns out to be Don Pieppo himself!

The only time the legal system was involved happened in 1888, when a woman named Frances McCann in Michigan befriended another woman who, during a fever, claimed to be Kate Bender. After recovering, the woman left town, prompting Mrs. McCann to follow her in search of the truth. During her investigation, McCann uncovered the story of Almira Griffith, a woman who had given birth to many children, all of whom were involved in criminal activities, including her daughter, Eliza. Mrs. McCann tracked Mrs. Griffith and Eliza to a jail in Niles, Michigan, where they had both accused each other of theft.

Mrs. McCann then traveled to Labette County to inform them that she had found both Ma and Kate Bender. She returned to Niles with Leroy Dick, a prominent town figure whose brother had been killed by the Benders, who confirmed their identities. In November 1889, Mrs. Griffith, Eliza, and her baby were taken to Kansas for trial.

A group of 16 individuals was assembled to identify if the "Griffiths" were really Ma and Kate Bender: seven confirmed their identities, six claimed they were not the same, and three were uncertain. The trial was slated for 1890, but their lawyer argued that Mrs. Griffith had been in jail for most of the time when the alleged crimes occurred. Additionally, what had happened to her German accent? The charges were dismissed, and the Griffiths, or whoever they were, boarded a train headed north, never to be heard from again.

Select Sources

Geary, Rick. *The Saga of the Bloody Benders: The Infamous Homicidal Family of Labette County, Kansas*. NBM Publishing, 2007.

Province, Charles M. *The Blood Stained Benders: More Evil Than You Know*. Independently Published, 2019.

Rudolp, Vance, and Allison Hardy. *Kate Bender, The Kansas Murderess: The Horrible History of an Arch Killer*. 1944. Republished, 2017.

York, Mary E. *The Bender Tragedy: Dedicated to the Memory of My Husband: Dr. William York*. Published by the author, 1875.

"The Bastardized Story of the Bloody Benders." *Internet Archaeology*, Medium.

"Bloody Bender house is up for sale in Kansas." CNN. 6 Feb. 2020.

"The Bloody Benders: America's First Family of Serial Killers." *CrimeReads*.

"The Benders – Kansas' Bloody Serial Killer Family." *Legends of America*.

"Mad Gasser of Mattoon." *Wikipedia*.

"Spring-heeled Jack." *Mythus Fandom Wiki*.

Daevas

Season 1, Episode 16

Title: Shadow

Dropped March 11, 2021

The symbol Dean found on the carpet is Zoroastrian and represents a Daeva, translated to "demon of darkness." The daeva sigil is likely a fictional creation but may represent the prophet Zoroaster with the letter Z. Dean, based on his research, determines that Zoroastrian demons are reminiscent of demonic pit bulls.

Zoroastrianism is the ancient religion of Persia (Iran), based on the teachings of the prophet Zarathustra (Zoroaster in Greek), who may have been born as early as 650 BC. This religion was dominant during the Persian empire from 559 BC to 651 AD. It was the most powerful religion at the time of Jesus, significantly influencing other faiths. It is still practiced worldwide, particularly in Iran and India, with around 140,000 followers.

The two primary texts of Zoroastrianism are the Gathas, which are sacred songs or odes, and the Avesta, which contains the central doctrines and creation myths. While Zoroastrianism shares similarities with Hinduism, it is fundamentally different because of its dualistic nature, characterized by the struggle between Good and Evil.

The term "devil" derives from the word "daeva," and the daevas profoundly influenced the angelologies and demonologies of Western religions. According to Zoroastrian beliefs, daevas were originally gods who could not distinguish between truth and lies. In Zoroastrian cosmology, daevas serve an evil god, Angra Mainyu (later known as Ahriman), who opposes a benevolent one, Ahura Mazda (later Ohrmazd). The daevas are depicted as beings who embody all diseases, sins, and humanity's various sufferings. When the prophet Zoroaster was born, the daevas hid beneath the earth, lurking and waiting to prey on the vulnerable. They are drawn to unclean places and often linger near exposed corpses. There are hordes of them, and the most powerful are referred to as "legion" in later texts, with each legion comprising 6,666 daevas. Although they are spirits, daevas can take on human forms. To ward off attacks from daevas, one should recite the Vendidad, a part of the Avesta. However, this ritual is only effective between sunset and sunrise.

Among the notable Daevas are:

Aka Manah embodies sensual desire and serves as the demon of lust, second in command to his father Ahriman.

Akoman, the second in command, means "evil mind" or "evil thought." Created from darkness, he carries a noticeable stench and targets individuals one by one, doing whatever it takes to corrupt them. He can only be dispelled by tricking him into believing he has succeeded.

Azhi-Dahak is a storm demon depicted as a man with two snakes growing from his shoulders, a result of Ahriman's kiss. In some descriptions, he has three heads and six eyes, and he is known to harm people and steal cattle.

Nai-Batar appears as a black shadow in the forms of a bat, predatory bird, raven, or wolf. Once summoned, this demon drains the power from others to empower his summoner. It enhances auras and aids emotional and spiritual vampirism.

Nasu, meaning "corpse," is the demon of bodily decomposition, decay, and pollution. Described as a monstrous speckled fly with backward-facing knees and a large stinger, Nasu can possess a corpse. If infected, a complicated nine-day cleansing ritual must be performed to restore purity.

Saurva, the chief, represents war and is characterized as immoral and ruthless. He commits acts that are evil, lawless, oppressive, tyrannical, and violent. To avoid becoming his victim, one must reject him in thought, deed, and word.

Select Sources

Bane, Thersa. Encyclopedia of Demons in World Religions and Cultures. McFarland, 2012.

Guiley, Rosemary Ellen. The Encyclopedia of Demons & Demonology. Facts on File, 2009.

Nathan Robert Brown. The Mythology of Supernatural. Berkley, 2011.

"aesma daeva." Metal Music Archives. metalmusicarchives.com/artist/aesma-daeva.

"Daeva." Genies Fandom Wiki. https://genies.fandom.com/wiki/Daeva.

"Spiritus Mundi: Definition, Lesson & Quiz." Study.com. https://study.com/academy/lesson/spiritus-mundi-definition-lesson-quiz.html.

"Zoroastrianism FAQ." Avesta.org. http://avesta.org/zfaq.html.

Tulpas

Season 1, Episode 17

Title: Hell House

Dropped: March 18, 2021

We have the Ghostfacers to thank for bringing the concept of a tulpa to life in this episode. At least we can thank them for something.

A tulpa, sometimes called a thought form, is a sentient being created through the power of concentrated thought, and is a concept practiced by Tibetan mystics. The sigil shown in the episode is a Sanskrit inscription adapted to the Tibetan script. It combines three phonetic symbols—tsa, la, and pa—to form the word *tulpa*. Traditionally, in addition to the sigil, monks would chant while collectively focusing on three distinct points of energy, directing that energy toward a specific idea or object until it converged into a physical manifestation. Typically, these objects were small, like a cup or a piece of fruit; it was rare for them to attempt to create a person.

The term *tulpa* began circulating in the West in 1929 with the publication Magic and Mystery in Tibet [*Mystiques et magiciens du Tibet*] by Belgian-French explorer Alexandra David-Néel. She reported observing the practice in Tibet and claimed to have created a tulpa of her own in the likeness of Friar Tuck. For many years, the concept of tulpa remained limited to Tibet and its mystics until 2009, when discussions about tulpas began to emerge on 4Chan, a forum where members started experimenting with the idea.

In 2012, a new group joined the tulpa conversation: the Bronies. The Bronies are a fandom of "My Little Pony," if you're somehow unfamiliar. The Bronies created a Reddit board dedicated to making tulpas based on their favorite characters, adopting the title of "tulpamancers." Soon after, fans of manga, anime, and gaming began to join in as well. Today, the tulpa subreddit boasts over 35,000 members, alongside a dedicated Discord server and various other websites and forums.

Tulpamancers perceive their imaginary companions as auditory hallucinations. Other senses, such as touch, emotions, and vision, can also play a role. The created tulpas are considered semi-permanent. Within the community, creating a tulpa is regarded as a lifelong commitment.

Tulpas typically take on human forms, though they can span a spectrum of humanoid variations, including gender-fluid, gender-neutral, or pan-ethnic traits. Fandom culture, particularly from fantasy-oriented genres, often leads to the creation of non-human Tulpas, such as elves or ponies. The creation of a tulpa is seen as a means to foster a relationship with an entity that can understand, accept, and bond with you on a level that transcends typical human interactions. A tulpa is an entity that operates independently and in parallel to one's consciousness, possessing its own thoughts, free will, emotions, and memories, but no supernatural powers.

Key Terms

Key terminology includes "forcing," which refers to concentrating your thoughts on your tulpa, willing it into existence, and using mental processes to facilitate its growth.

"Mindvoice" denotes what is heard in your head when you or your tulpa speaks or thinks.

"Plural" describes a state of having multiple personalities within a single body. At the same time, "singlet" refers to a person with no tulpas or alternate personalities.

"Wonderlands" are mental environments where hosts and tulpas can interact without having to manifest the tulpa in the physical world. A wonderland can be revisited repeatedly, although it may evolve and can range from a small room to an entire universe or even a void of nothingness.

When it comes to the topic of sex, it can be controversial within the community. Linkzelda, the anonymous author of a Tulpa creation guide, noted, "Imagine how that would make them feel. That they were only created as a sex doll." One user also expressed almost revulsion at the idea, "I never understood the sexual attraction to tulpas. To me, they are my friends yet not friends, me yet not me, family, yet not family. Of course, I made them visually appealing young ladies, but it would feel akin to coveting your own sisters." If you're interested, you can also check out r/TulpasGoneWild, where users share pictures of their conquests. However, since no one else can see them, the message board is filled with images of empty beds and vacant rooms.

Samuel Veissière, an anthropologist and researcher in transcultural psychiatry and cognitive science, reached out to the tulpamancer community at McGill University in Montreal to explore the mental, cultural, and therapeutic aspects of tulpamancy. Tulpamancers consistently reported positive experiences, including increased happiness and greater confidence in challenging social situations, after interaction with their tulpa companions. The tulpamancers reported that loneliness and social anxiety motivated them to engage in the practice, which in turn led to positive changes in their social lives and offline interactions, as well as a variety of new, unusual, yet largely positive sensory experiences. In another survey of tulpamancers, 32 out of 57 respondents (56%) indicated that they had been diagnosed with a mental or neurodevelopmental disorder, with the most common diagnoses being depressive disorders, anxiety disorders, and autism spectrum disorder. For individuals grappling with disorders that involve delusions and misperceptions, the tulpa can serve as a voice of reason during moments of irrationality.

As today's culture is not quite accepting of mental experiences like tulpa creation, the "fringeness" of the tulpamancy subculture creates a sense of solidarity that contributes to a general understanding of reward and positivity. The perception of tulpas as intimate and trustworthy companions may help explain the association between tulpas and improvements in mental health. The majority of tulpamancers develop strong, intimate bonds with their systemmates. Additionally, tulpamancers coped well with challenges such as pandemic quarantines, as they were accustomed to being alone and had developed coping mechanisms that allowed them to entertain themselves.

Select Sources

"1.17 Hell House - Super-wiki." Supernatural Wiki. http://www.supernaturalwiki.com/1.17_Hell_House

"Daring to Hear Voices | Psychology Today." Psychology Today. 12 Apr. 2016. https://www.psychologytoday.com/us/blog/culture-mind-and-brain/201604/daring-hear-voices

"Dr. Samuel Veissière quoted in Washington Post | Department of Psychiatry - McGill University." McGill University. https://www.mcgill.ca/psychiatry/channels/news/dr-samuel-veissiere-quoted-washington-post-327431

"The Internet's Newest Subculture Is All About Creating Imaginary Friends." Vice. https://www.vice.com/en/article/exmqzz/tulpamancy-internet-subculture-892

"Leviathan Cross Meaning And Symbolism: Sulfur Symbol AKA Infinity/Satanic Cross And Sigil Tattoo Ideas." Symbols and Meanings. https://symbolsandmeanings.net/leviathan-cross-meaning-symbolism-origin-satanic-satans-cross/

r/Tulpas. Reddit. https://www.reddit.com/r/Tulpas/

r/TulpasGoneWild. Reddit. https://www.reddit.com/r/TulpasGoneWild/

Tulpa.org.

Tulpa.info. https://www.tulpa.info/

Tulpas and Mental Health: A Study of Non-Traumagenic Plural Experiences. Psychology and Behavioral Science. http://pubs.sciepub.com/rpbs/5/2/1/index.html

What is a brony? https://www.whatisabrony.com/

https://gist.github.com/cmcsun/5341046#file-entire-guide

https://www.imdb.com/name/nm0518910/bio?ref_=nm_ov_bio_sm

Shtrigas

Season 1, Episode 18

Title: Something Wicked

Dropped: March 25, 2021

The shtriga lore in this episode gets somewhat close to the real lore, but at least they left out the part about spitting into the sick kids' mouths.

From Albanian folklore, a shtriga is a vampiric witch known for sucking blood, especially that of children. The term "shtriga" is also commonly used to refer to a witch, specifically a stereotype of an old, ugly woman who casts spells. The male equivalents are shtrigu or shtrigan. By day, the shtriga appear human, but at night, they transform into flying creatures resembling bugs, flies, or moths.
The shtriga legends likely originate from the Roman *strix*, with the key distinction being the belief that the shtriga can change into various flying creatures, unlike the strix, which is limited to bird forms. Still, the lore about their

shape-shifting is mixed: in some accounts, they also transform into insects or moths to enter through keyholes and suck blood, leaving the person pale, feverish, and ultimately dying. In the Balkans, they are known as Vjeshtitza. People often kill moths, saying, "Perhaps it is a vjeshtitza."

In one folk tale, a young, pregnant married woman craved wine, but the family was too poor to buy any. Her mother-in-law was a shtriga, who stripped the woman naked and anointed her with a salve while saying magic words shrinking her to the size of a bee. "Go to the cellar of so and so and crawl through the keyhole and drink all you want. But be careful not to say the name of God." The young woman went to the cellar and drank her fill, but in her drunk enthusiasm exclaimed, "Thank God!" and all at once became her natural size. So she's naked and likely hammered in the cellar and had to stay there until the next day, when the landlord opened the door to find, to his surprise, a naked young woman. He was surprised but nice and gave her a coat and believed whatever story she told him.

Shtriga primarily prey on infants and children, feeding on spiritus vitae, or breath of life, at night. Those affected by the Shtriga often slip into a coma, leaving them vulnerable to diseases, which can result in death from conditions like pneumonia. Victims can be saved by catching the witch that has been sucking blood and making the shtriga spit in the victim's mouth. A clear sign of a shtriga's presence is a multitude of sick children, as well as the unusual occurrence of a young girl's hair turning white. If a woman's hair turns white by the age of 20, she is often believed to be a witch.

To protect against shtrigas, an amulet can be made from a silver coin dipped in shtriga's blood. Luckily, shtrigas tend to drink excessive amounts of blood and often retreat to the woods to vomit up the excess. To craft the amulet, follow a suspected shtriga into the woods, dip the coin in the shtriga's blood vomit, then wrap it in the handkerchief and carry it next to your person, and the shtriga will leave you alone.

An additional protection method comes from folklore suggesting that witches could sail the seas in boats made from eggshells. On the first of March, it is tradition in Albania to smash eggshells for protection. Another safeguard is garlic, which was traditionally worn around children's necks to prevent interaction with the shtriga and, probably, any potential friends. During the first week of March, people would hang scissors, combs for carding wool, black thread tied in knots, and unspecified acidic fruits on their doors to protect homes and prevent shtrigas from causing harm.

Shtriga can only be killed in human form. They can be captured by creating a cross with pig bones and fastening it to a church, rendering the Shtriga unable to escape. Directions from that point are unclear.

Select Sources

"1.18 Something Wicked." Supernatural Wiki. http://www.supernaturalwiki.com/ 1.18_Something_Wicked.

Durham, M. (1910). High Albania and its Customs in 1908. The Journal of the Royal Anthropological Institute of Great Britain and Ireland, 40, 453-472. doi:10.2307/2843266

Durham, M. (1923). 121. Of Magic, Witches and Vampires in the Balkans. Man, 23, 189-192. doi:10.2307/2788569
"Shtriga." The Demoniacal. 2010. https:// thedemoniacal.blogspot.com/2010/07/ shtriga.html.

"Shtriga." Lots of Lore. https:// lotsoflore.blogspot.com/p/shtriga.html.

"Shtriga." Metal Archives. https://www.metal- archives.com/bands/Shtriga/68384.

"Shtriga." WikiMili. https://wikimili.com/en/ Shtriga.

"Striga." Wikipedia. https://en.wikipedia.org/wiki/Striga.

Corpsewood Manor

Season 1, Episode 19

Title: Provenance

Dropped: April 1, 2021

Searching for haunted paintings like the one in this episode led me to Corpsewood Manor, which is a fascinating story about an eccentric couple I wish I'd known in real life.

Trigger warning for murder, violence, and animal murder.

The story of Corpsewood Manor is really the story of Charles Scudder and Joey Odom. Charles was an intellectual, which could make him seem aloof, but that was just his way. His sense of style was evident when he purchased a west Chicago mansion in the 1950s because it reminded him of the Addams Family cartoons. At the time, he lived there with his four sons from his second wife, Bourtai, while studying for his graduate degree at Loyola's School of Medicine. Then he met Joey Odom in a bookstore. Joey was the opposite of Charles; he had dropped out of school in the fifth grade, but was street-smart. Their differences worked, and Joey became Charles' live-in cook and housekeeper.

In 1964, Charles earned his PhD in Pharmacology, specializing in psychopharmacology and behavior. Then he became the assistant director of the Institute for the Study of Mind, Drugs, and Behavior at Loyola. Some of his academic peers deemed him eccentric because of his purple-and-red hair, flamboyant clothing, and his pet monkey. Remember a time when it was extraordinary to have colored hair? Also, his mansion featured a pink gargoyle fountain.

Charles was musically inclined; he learned to play the harp, and the Chicago Orchestra invited him to join. He also created paintings, charcoal drawings, and stained glass. However, his creative side waged war with the politics and rigidity of academia and science. In a letter to a friend, he said, "I came to feel a scientist indulges in more than endless measurement. He must speculate. He must dream. He must find that which is beyond understanding." This sentiment naturally led him to explore the esoteric and occult.

By the 1970s, Charles' sons had grown into adulthood, leaving him and Odom as the only occupants of the large house. Charles received a modest inheritance but felt overwhelmed by the weight of his mansion, which had transformed into a money pit. He described it as "more like a mausoleum, a tomb requiring care, cleaning, and endless costly repairs," and not quite the Addams Family dream. The overwhelming burden of taxes and utility bills, and the decline of his old neighborhood, led him to create a new plan. He envisioned a new life in a hilly region that offered the charm of four distinct seasons without harsh winters, along with a dependable supply of pure water and wood for heating and cooking. Most importantly, he sought isolation.

To find the perfect spot, Charles studied geological survey maps of southern states. He reached out to the presidents of local realty boards. One responded, informing him of 40 affordable acres of hardwood trees nestled in the Appalachian foothills, surrounded by national forest land.

In 1976, on his fiftieth birthday, Charles resigned from his teaching position, auctioned off all the furniture and possessions he didn't care about, gave away his electrical appliances, sold the mansion, and arranged for a moving company to handle the items he wanted to keep. Together with Joey and their two English mastiffs, they set off for their "kingdom." The two massive dogs were incredibly lovable, one affectionately named Beelzebub, after the prince of devils, and the other Arsinath, likely inspired by a Lovecraft character. Charles also brought along some military-grade LSD and skulls from his job, as you do.

The journey to their stake in land began amid a blizzard, and they soon found themselves lost as they tried to locate their new property. Life before GPS was a living hell. Finally, they found the road leading to their house, which bore the carcass of a rotting horse, earning it the name Dead Horse Road. The trees that succumbed to the blizzard inspired the nickname Corpsewood Road. Once they arrived, they built their house from scratch, sleeping outside with their antiques, statues, books, and Charles' big ass harp sheltered under a tarp.

When visitors came by during the construction and brought fruit, Charles would make wine from it, naming it after the person who brought it. During this time, Jerry suffered a serious head injury in an accident involving someone else's jeep, which seriously slowed him down. Charles nursed him back to health while continuing to build the house.

The house itself was arguably amazing, made of curved bricks, three layers thick with two-inch-wide air spaces between them for insulation. Measuring only 44 by 16 feet, it featured a retractable drawbridge that connected the main house to a sundeck above the entrance gazebo. There, they would drink tea while Charles played the harp in the moonlight. It was also where the pink gargoyle sat and probably came to life. A sign on the road leading to the property read, "Beware of the Thing." Some claimed it served as a warning about a demon Scudder invoked to protect the estate. However, I suspect Charles still really loved the Addams Family.

Inside, the house was adorned with occult art, most notably a black-and-gold statue of Mephistopheles and a stained-glass piece depicting Baphomet created by Charles.

Locals sometimes called the Corpsewood Manor the "devil worshippers' house," and that is slightly accurate, as Charles was a confirmed member of the Anton LaVey-era Church of Satan. Occasionally, Charles would introduce himself and Joey as Satanists, prompting Joey to quip, "Speak for yourself, smartass; I'm Catholic." Charles even adorned the side of the jeep with giant white pentacles. From the various sources I've explored, here's my take: Charles was a scientist and an atheist who appreciated the Church of Satan (which was largely atheistic at the time) for its hedonistic philosophy and nonjudgmental views on sexuality. He was also interested in metaphysics and the occult—essentially, a goth without the eyeliner. Who knows, he likely had eyeliner on.

The other part of the house we need to discuss is the "chicken coop." This building, separate from the main house, consisted of three levels. The first level was a literal chicken coop; the second housed a pornographic library; and the third level, known as "the pink room," was where Charles hosted parties, featuring some mattresses and S&M gear.

Although they generally stayed away from town, Charles and Joey often welcomed guests, and Charles entertained them with his homemade wine. They also had visitors from pen pals Charles connected with through gay trade magazines, including some ex-convicts. Sketchy, but essentially, they were living their best life in the woods.

Fast forward to the year 1982, when things took a turn. Kenneth Avery Brock, a petty criminal, started hanging out at Corpsewood Manor. He was known to get drunk and was likely engaging in some sexual encounter with Charles. Brock convinced his roommate, Tony West, to join him at Corpsewood, proclaiming Charles and Joey cool. Avery and Tony arrived to meet Charles and the two dogs—at that time, Arsinath was still alive, but Beelzebub had passed, and their new mastiff was named Lucifer.

As they all got drunk, it is alleged that Charles pleasured Avery and then offered the same to Tony, who declined. On the way back to town, Tony and Avery made a plot, convinced that Charles and Jerry had considerable money and valuables, and devised a plan to kill and rob them.
The two put that plan into motion on the night of December 12, 1982. To add to the chaos, Avery and Tony picked up Joey Wells and his friend Teresa Hudgins, who was only 18, and headed out to Corpsewood Manor.

According to Teresa Hudgins, the group made their way up to the pink room while Charles went to fetch some wine. The group passed around bottles of wine, though Teresa later admitted she only pretended to drink and didn't believe Charles had any either. Avery decided to go downstairs for something and returned with a .22 rifle. He set it down, and Charles, thinking it was a joke, infamously said, "Bang bang." Charles got up to adjust a lamp, and Avery grabbed him, pressed a knife to his throat, and demanded money. Charles repeatedly insisted he didn't have any, then was gagged, and his hands and feet were bound. They pulled down the gag to ask questions, including who else was in the house, to which Charles replied, "Joey." He desperately tried to talk them out of the situation, hoping it was all just a game, saying things like, "I'll go along with your game. What kind of game do you want to play?"

Meanwhile, Teresa and Joey escaped down the ladder and attempted to start the car, but it wouldn't turn over. Tony chased after them with the gun. They returned inside, where Avery held the knife on Charles, who had fallen silent. Avery took the gun and killed both Joey and the dogs. Charles began to moan and cry, and Avery escorted him down the ladder and into the house, past Joey's body, causing Charles to lose control, trying to kneel beside him, but not allowed. Avery pushed Charles into the library, where he was pressed further for information on the location of money and valuables.

Even while distraught, Charles checked on Teresa and asked if she was alright; however, Tony and Avery forced him back into a chair, and Tony shot him in the forehead twice more, taunting, "Now tell me by God that I don't have the guts to kill somebody." Despite his wounds, Charles still struggled to stand to reach Joey but ultimately fell and died.

The house was ransacked for anything of value. They attempted to take Charles' harp, but it wouldn't fit in their car. Avery went to check on Jerry and discovered he wasn't dead, and he shot him again. In the end, the thieves escaped with a handful of dimes and nickels, some jewelry, a camera, a stereo, silver candelabras, a leather jacket, and a gold-plated dagger. They also took Odom's Jeep, which still had the white pentacles painted on the door. They briefly considered burning the house but decided it would attract too much attention, so they drove away instead.

Avery and Tony went on the run, trying to reach Mexico. At a rest stop in Mississippi, they shot and killed a Navy lieutenant who was taking a nap for $30 and stole his Toyota. Eventually, they ditched the Jeep in Louisiana. In Austin, a hitchhiker they picked up directed them to a pawn shop, where they sold the camera and stereo for $200. After securing a motel room, they celebrated by visiting a topless bar. Their night took a turn when they got into a fight and separated. Still, both eventually returned and surrendered to the police. Teresa had already come forward and informed the authorities about what had happened.

During Tony West's trial, Tony claimed Charles laced the wine with LSD, which supposedly justified their actions. The state tested the wine and found no traces of LSD, a defense which only emerged after acid was discovered during a search of their home. Both Tony and Avery went to prison.

Now, let's go back to the house. While agents were clearing the property, they found a painting, a portrait—perhaps a self-portrait—depicting a man gagged and bound in a chair with five gunshot wounds to the head, which aligns with the autopsy findings for Charles. The painting eventually found its way to a private collector, along with the statue, the harp, and the gargoyle.

The property of Corpsewood Manor is rumored to be haunted and cursed. Over the years, much of it has burned down due to a couple of arson fires. Many who have taken items from the property, such as rosebushes and bricks, have experienced terrible luck and returned them out of fear. There are numerous tales of people hearing harps, seeing glowing eyes from dogs, and even hearing gunshots.

One of my favorite stories from Amy Petulla's book is about her experience after finishing the original manuscript. While getting a massage, she shared her story with the masseuse, who revealed that he had visited Corpsewood once with friends on a dare. When they arrived, they found no other cars but noticed two men sitting in lawn chairs where the house once stood. The men appeared to be in their forties and returned to that spot every year on the same day. They spoke about what had happened there before the boys ventured into the woods to explore. When they returned, the men had vanished. Upon hearing their descriptions, Amy went to her car and retrieved the manuscript with photos of Charles. The masseuse's jaw dropped as he recognized the blonde man, noting that he looked identical to the image, right down to his style of dress. I like to think that Charles, Joey, and the dogs are enjoying their afterlife in the woods with Corpsewood Manor.

Select Sources

"Corpsewood Manor." Atlas Obscura,_https://www.atlasobscura.com/places/corpsewood-manor.

"Corpsewood Manor: True Crime Like No Other." Winter Watch, December 19, 2019,

"Castle in the Country." Mother Earth News, https://www.motherearthnews.com/homesteading-and-livestock/castle-in-the-country-zmaz81mazraw.

The Corpsewood Manor Murders in North Georgia (True Crime) Paperback August 8, 2016 by Amy Petulla (Author).

"Death was the final visitor to home o 'devil worhsiper's'," Andy Knott. Chicago Tribune Sun, Jan 02, 1983, p. 4.

"The Cold-Blooded Killing of the Gay 'Satanists' of Corpsewood Manor." Investigation Discovery, https://www.investigationdiscovery.com/crimefeed/

crime-history/the-cold-blooded-killing-of-the-gay-satanists-of-corpsewood-mano.

"The Horrifying Backstory of Corpsewood Manor." Grunge, https://www.grunge.com/233391/the-horrifying-backstory-of-corpsewood-manor/.

Grave Eating Vampires

Season 1, Episode 20

Title: Dead Man's Blood

Dropped April 8, 2021

It's really hard knowing you are going to have vampires in dozens of episodes to come. Thankfully there is a lot to be said about vampires. The written version is not as much fun as me making "posthumous chewing sounds" like an ASMR goddess as was done on the podcast recording.

Grave-eating

Before we get into vampires, one of the earliest "medical" studies of post-mortem behavior of the dead or undead, as the case may be, was the 1679 empirical study by Phillip Rohr on 'grave-eating,' also known as manducation or posthumous chewing. His research detailed instances where open graves revealed that the deceased had been consuming their own shrouds, cloths, and occasionally even their own limbs and bowels. Disturbing sounds accompanied this phenomenon, with the dead reported to have "grunted, gibbered, and squeaked under the ground," which is only slightly better than "nom nom nom."

Peter Plogojowitz

In 1725, the villagers of the northeastern Serbian village of Kisilova (now known as Kiisiljevo) begged their Ottoman rulers for protection from a rampaging vampire. Still, the rulers dismissed the villagers' fears, prompting many to flee. When the nightmare returned, the villagers knew who the vampire was: Peter Plogojowitz. You see, though Peter had died ten weeks earlier, he had been seen around the village. His wife was the first to see him when Peter came home asking for his shoes, which she gave him before he departed. Things escalated quickly, and in the following week, at least nine individuals claimed that Peter had attacked them, throttling them before draining blood from their stomachs and throats. Each victim died within 24 hours. Returning home once more, Peter demanded food. His wife cowered in fear, while their son refused to comply. In a fit of rage, Peter killed his son, and his wife ran in terror.

The villagers approached the Austrian official in charge, an Imperial Provisor named Frombald, demanding that he eliminate the vampire or they would all leave. This placed Frombald in a difficult position: if the villagers abandoned the village under his watch, it would reflect poorly on him, yet if he were to dig up the "vampire," he would risk being ridiculed by his superiors. He made the decision, and Frombald went to the caves with the local priest and a group of villagers to dig up Peter. Local officials reported on the exhumation, "First of all, I did not detect the slightest odor that is characteristic of the dead. The body was completely fresh, except for the nose, which had somewhat deteriorated. The hair and beard—even the nails, which had fallen away—had regrown. The old skin, somewhat whitish, had peeled away, revealing a new, fresh layer underneath. Not without astonishment, I noticed some fresh blood in his mouth."

The villagers drove a metal stake through his chest, and Frombald witnessed what appeared to be fresh blood pumping from the wound, as well as from the body's nose, mouth, and ears. The villagers then took the corpse and incinerated it on a pyre. Frombald's superiors affirmed he had made the right decision. Upon returning to Belgrade, the commander and his officers convened again and prepared a report concluding that Peter Plogojowitz had indeed been a vampire. This report was published by Wienerisches Diarium, a Viennese newspaper now known as Die Wiener Zeitung.

Arnod Paole (variously Arnond, Arnont, or Arnaold Paul)

In 1727, Arnod Paole returned home from his service in the Austrian army to his Serbian village of Meduegna, near Belgrade. While stationed in Turkish Serbia, he reportedly told his fiancée that a vampire had plagued his regiment. A group of men, including Paole himself, had been sent to find and destroy the creature. He claimed to have killed the vampire and, in some stories, ate dirt from its grave and smeared himself with its blood to prevent being turned; in others, this act caused his infection. He settled down as a farmer and became engaged to a local girl. However, his neighbors noticed a subtle change in his character since his return from the army.

Tragically, before his wedding could take place, his hay wagon overturned and killed him. Three weeks after he was buried, several townspeople reported sightings of Arnold Paole, claiming he had entered their bedrooms at night. Four of those who complained later died from an unidentified illness. The specter of Arnold Paole was blamed for these deaths, and the word "vampire" began to be whispered in the area. Forty days post-burial, the villagers opened Arnold's grave, revealing an undecayed body. Fresh blood oozed from his eyes, nose, and ears, while his shirt, shroud, and coffin were soaked in blood. Although his fingernails had fallen off, they were replaced by new growths, and his hair appeared significantly longer. To put an end to the terror, townspeople drove a stake through his heart (one account mentions it was made of whitethorn), eliciting a loud groan or shriek from him as fresh blood gushed forth. They subsequently burned his body and scattered the ashes in the grave. The four deceased individuals were also staked and cremated. However, this was not the conclusion of the vampire saga in the town.

Four years later, in 1731, more people began to die, prompting authorities to exhume graves where more corpses were found unrotted. A medical team, including an epidemiologist, a military surgeon, and two medical officers, was called in to investigate. The team discovered that the so-called vampire corpses were being decapitated and cremated. Reports indicated that "Arnold Paole attacked not only people but also livestock, draining their blood. As locals consumed meat from these animals, several vampires emerged among them." Paole had not only vampirized humans but also sheep, and this consumption spread the pestilence. Vampire sheep!
Among the people accused of being vampires were seven women (two of whom had babies), two soldiers, a servant, two teenage boys, and children aged 9 and 10. Notably, one woman bore a mark on her neck; during that era, the signature of a vampire was not the puncture wounds of fangs, but rather signs of strangulation. This particular woman had a

contusion on the right side of her neck beneath the ear, a bloodshot blue mark about the length of a finger.

The military surgeon wrote a report detailing the case of Arnod Paole from five years prior. The report was endorsed, signed, and published, quickly sweeping across Europe. Meanwhile, the epidemiologist's father, also a doctor, published an article in a weekly medical journal claiming that a medical plague was rampant in Serbia, causing the dead to rise from their graves and attack the living. This journal went on to publish more than 17 articles on vampirism in 1732. In the years 1732 to 1733, twelve books and four dissertations on the subject were released, and interest continued to grow. Vampires began to be seen as metaphors for political rulers and imperialistic oppressors, featuring prominently in various satires. The cultural impact was evident when, in 1751, the Earl of Sandwich named his bay gelding racehorse "Vampire."

Select Sources

"The Case of Arnold Paole: Real-Life Vampire Story." Anomalien._https://anomalien.com/the-case-of-arnold-paole-real-life-vampire-story/.

"Serbian Vampire Peter Plogojowitz." Wizzley. https://wizzley.com/serbian-vampire-peter-plogojowitz/.

"The Colt." Supernatural Wiki. http://www.supernaturalwiki.com/The_Colt.

"The Legendary Arnold Paole." Vampires.com. https://www.vampires.com/the-legendary-arnold-paole/.

The Vampire: A New History Groom, Nick 2018.

"Trillium." Wikipedia. Wikimedia Foundation. https://en.wikipedia.org/wiki/Trillium.

"Vampire Peter Plogojowitz." The Unexplained Mysteries. July 24, 2017. http://theunexplainedmysteries.com/2017/07/24/vampire-peter-plogojowitz/.

Holy Water

Season 1, Episode 21

Title: Salvation

Dropped April 15, 2021

Have you ever really stopped to think about where the Winchesters get their holy water from? Do they steal it from churches? Do they make their own?

This will focus on the Judeo-Christian version of Holy Water, which does appear in the King James Bible. In one instance, God provided Moses with a recipe or spell to prove a woman's faithfulness when her husband accused her of cheating: the man was to put holy water in an earthen vessel, then throw in some dirt from the pavement of the tabernacle. The woman in question should be given the new extra holy water to drink; if she weren't cheating, nothing would happen. However, if she were guilty, she would be cursed, and her belly would begin to swell while her thighs would start to rot.

In the Roman Catholic and Orthodox Christian traditions, holy water is water blessed by a priest or bishop. That is what we think of for use on demons or vampires, depending on what mythology you are talking about.

There are other types of holy water:

- Saint or Non-Liturgical Holy Water: This is sometimes less potent than traditional holy water; it is found in "holy wells" or other water sources associated with Saints.
- Gregorian Holy Water: Traditional holy water that has been mixed with wine, salt, and ashes.
- Relic or Sanctified Holy Water: This water becomes holy by dipping holy relics into it or by touching them if the dip would harm the relic.

How to make your own slightly holy water according to WikiHow:

1. Get water
2. Find a clean vessel to put it in
3. You can put salt in it, but the salt has to be exorcized or consecrated first
4. Then you bless it with some Latin. Well, there isn't a rule that it has to be Latin.

Or you could buy it on Amazon, because of course you can.

Select Sources

Brown, Nathan Robert. The Mythology of Supernatural. 2011.

"Holy Water." Catholic Encyclopedia. https://www.catholic.com/encyclopedia/holy-water.

"Make Your Own Holy Water." wikiHow. https://www.wikihow.com/Make-Your-Own-Holy-Water.

"Holy Water." ReligionFacts. https://religionfacts.com/holy-water.

"Nike Air Max 97 'Jesus Shoes' Filled with Holy Water Selling for $4,000." CBS News, 11 Oct. 2019. https://www.cbsnews.com/news/nike-air-max-97-jesus-shoes-filled-with-holy-water-selling-for-4000-2019-10-11/.

"Fatima's Little-Known Miracles with Earth and Water." National Catholic Register, https://www.ncregister.com/blog/fatima-s-little-known-miracles-with-earth-and-water.

"Peter Popoff's Miracle Spring Water." Truth in Advertising, https://www.truthinadvertising.org/peter-popoffs-miracle-spring-water/.

Direct From Lourdes. Accessed 10 December 2025. https://www.directfromlourdes.com/i.

Water from Jordan River with Certificate, Holy Water for House Blessing. Amazon, Accessed 10 December 2025. https://www.amazon.com/Water-Jordan-Certificate-House-Blessing/dp/B01KYGB22E/ref=sr_1_2?dchild=1&keywords=holy+water&qid=1618340608&sr=8-2.

The Devil's Trap and the Key of Solomon

Season 1, Episode 22

Title: Devil's Trap

Dropped April 22, 2021

How could I not talk about the devil's trap symbol? But to do that, we talk about the Key of Solomon.

These days, most probably don't associate Judaism much with magic, but around the time of Jesus, the Jewish people of the region had a significant reputation as magicians. Plus, let's not forget the mysticism of the Kabbalah. Several scrolls and other "lost texts" are believed to hold the wisdom of Moses, who is said to have acquired magical knowledge during his time in Egypt, which would explain the parting of the seas and the dropping of plagues.

King Solomon, the son of David, ruled Israel in the 10th century BCE and is revered for his wisdom in Judaism and Christianity, while in Islam, he is acknowledged as a prophet. King Solomon completed the Holy Temple in Jerusalem, which housed the Ark of the Covenant. This temple holds significant influence among the Freemasons, as do many symbols and sigils derived from the Key of Solomon. King Solomon is best known for the dramatic story of the proposed division of a baby.

In the first century CE, a Jewish historian provided the earliest depiction of Solomon as a magician, claiming that Solomon authored 3,000 books, including works on spells and exorcisms.

The first magic book commonly attributed to Solomon is the Testament of Solomon. Written in Greek and likely originating in Babylonia or Egypt, this work recounts the legend of demons blocking the construction of Solomon's temple by vampirizing his favorite worker and draining his soul through his thumb. To combat this, Solomon prayed, and the angel Michael presented him with a magical ring from God, which he could use to bind demons with the Seal of Solomon. The nature of this seal varies by interpretation and can be represented as a pentagram, a hexagon, a circle, or even words. The British Library holds some fascinating Seal of Solomon rings, dating to the 5th or 6th centuries. With the power granted to him by the ring, Solomon essentially commanded demons to build the temple for him. Solomon would subdue demons by pointing it at their chests—or possibly throwing it at them—and yelling, "Solomon summons you!" Through the ring, he compelled demons to appear and reveal their powers and weaknesses. Demons manifested in various forms, including dog-headed beings, humans, bulls, dragons with bird faces, beasts, and sphinxes. Solomon categorized 36 lower-level demons responsible for diseases and strife.

Some of the demons Solomon learned about include:
Oropel: who causes sore throats and mucus
Phobothel: causes loosening of the tendons
Rhyx Nathotho: he causes knee problems and can be repelled if you write "Phounebiel" on a piece of papyrus

Rhyx Axesbuth: causes diarrhea and hemorrhoids. If he is adjured in pure wine given to the sufferer, he retreats.
Rhyx Physikoreth: causes choking on fish bones. If you put fish bones on the breasts of the afflicted person, he retreats.

The most influential book attributed to Solomon is the *Clavicula Solomonis*, or the Key of Solomon. Additionally, another grimoire emerged in the 17th century, known as the Lemegeton, or the *Lesser Key of Solomon*. This grimoire provides instructions for evoking the 72 demons captured by Solomon, and it generally explains how to conjure and control demons and perform various acts for personal gain, such as invoking love, punishing enemies, becoming invisible, and dealing with thieves.

The oldest known existing copy is in the *BNF Ital. 1524*, an Italian manuscript dating back to 1446, although it is believed to have been translated from a Latin text housed in the library of Duke Filippo Maria in Pavia in 1426. Early Greek versions from around the fifteenth century exist, and the work has been translated into many languages. It was tradition to copy versions by hand, partly because handwritten copies were believed to hold more power. This manual copying also makes it challenging to determine what constituted an authoritative version. Some works bore Solomon's name but were merely magic scrapbooks or compilations of spells aimed at seducing women, controlling witches, performing exorcisms, summoning spirits, and more.

The most widely read English translation was compiled in 1889 by British occultist Samuel Liddell MacGregor Mathers, a founder of the Hermetic Order of the Golden Dawn, a secret society dedicated to magic. He used various manuscripts and languages, translating them in a manner he likely favored, even omitting love spells.

In Mathers's edition, the grimoire is divided into two parts. Book I contains conjurations, invocations, and curses to summon and constrain spirits of the dead and demons, compelling them to fulfill the operator's will. It also provides instructions on locating stolen items, becoming invisible, and gaining favor and love, among other things.

The book also guides magicians on appropriate attire, like the following instructions for what to wear while performing ritual work:
"Shoes or boots should be crafted from white leather, adorned with the symbols and characters of the art. These shoes must be made during the days of fasting and abstinence, specifically during the nine days leading up to the operation. During this time, the necessary instruments should also be prepared—polished, brightened, and cleaned. Additionally, the master of the art should wear a crown made of virgin paper, inscribed with four names: JEHOVA in the front, ADONAI at the back, EL on the right, and GIBOR on the left." The book also includes sections on the experiment of invisibility and instructions on how to hinder a sportsman from killing any game.

Hundreds of copies and versions still exist today. Its popularity is evidenced by its frequent inclusion among the books that led to the condemnation of individuals, often priests, during the Inquisition, resulting in many copies burned. Throughout history, it has experienced various surges in popularity, particularly during the Renaissance, the French exploration of the occult, and the rise of Spiritualism and Freemasonry. The Key of Solomon has significantly influenced modern magick and pagan rituals. The magical seals contributed to numerous images found in grimoires, many of which appear to control demons or even to influence the logo of this podcast.

Select Sources

"AF-253." British Museum._https://www.britishmuseum.org/collection/object/H_AF-253.

"The Grimoires of Biblical King: The Magical Treatise of Solomon and The Key of Solomon." Ancient Origins. Ancient-origins.net.

"Jefferson City, Missouri." Wikipedia. https://en.wikipedia.org/wiki/Jefferson_City%2C_Missouri.

"Key of Solomon." Wikipedia. En.wikipedia.org.

"King Solomon's Grimoires." Esoteric Archives. Esotericarchives.com.

"The Lesser Key of Solomon: The Dedication." Sacred Texts. Sacred-texts.com.

"S. L. MacGregor Mathers." The Hermetic Order of the Golden Dawn: A Golden Dawn

Magical Tradition.
Goldendawnancientmysteryschool.com.

"Solomon: Legendary Wisdom." Britannica.

"Spirits of Solomon." Occult World. Occult-world.com.

Wikimedia Commons. File: Tree of life bahir Hebrew.svg.